The Cowboy Stuntman

Secrets of a Long and Exciting Career

By Buckskin Jack McElrath

RUSHMORE HOUSE PUBLISHING
1997

Published by
RUSHMORE HOUSE PUBLISHING
Sioux Falls, South Dakota 57101

ISBN 0-9624593-5-6

Library of Congress
Catalog Card Number 97-68793

ALL RIGHTS RESERVED

Copyright © 1997 by
RUSHMORE HOUSE PUBLISHING

FIRST EDITION

Edited by:
Jaciel Keltgen-Pierson

Cover collage painted by Ray Kelly

Printed by Pine Hill Press, Inc.
Freeman, South Dakota
Manufactured in the United States of America

TABLE OF CONTENTS

Back to the Beginning. 1

The Rodeo Years 6

The Military Doesn't Put Up With Many Stunts . . 37

Skydogging Isn't As Easy As It Looks 42

How To Crash a Stunt Car 45

Stunts, Stunts & More Stunts 49

My Mind Works As Hard As My Body 53

Look Out, Kirk Douglas! 67

It Wasn't All Wine and Roses 71

Dead Men Don't Make Much Money 78

One Minute I Was Riding Steers and the
Next Minute Rubbing Elbows With Stars 97

Working Girls and Working Guys 102

All Work and No Play Makes Jack a Dull Cowboy 111

And the Winner Is... 115

Excuse Me, But Did Somebody Mention the Word
DANGER? 118

How To Get Your Face on TV 121

To Tell A Good Story You've Got to Lead An
Interesting Life 124

Recalling Events 130

This Big Go-Round Called Life 137

THE COWBOY STUNTMAN
Secrets of a Long and Exciting Career

By Buckskin Jack McElrath

Foreword
September 14, 1996, Sioux Falls, SD

In my more than six decades of living, I've survived thousands of dangerous stunts, married and divorced three times, met celebrities with kind hearts and many more without any heart at all, seen how drugs can ravage lives, appeared on TV as well as in sensational tabloid newspapers and pretty much had the time of my life.

It's been a good ride. I had a farm boy start in Moville, Iowa, and spent time in Sioux Falls, South Dakota, as well as Las Vegas, Nevada, and countless fairs – like the fine Ozark Empire Fair in Springfield, MO – and rodeos in between. And then there were the TV shows, movies, bull rides, saddle bronc rides, steer wrestling, car crashes, motorcycle jumps, 200-foot-long fireslides, carefully timed jumps from low-flying airplanes onto running steers, a stint in the Air Force and even running an 8-minute mile at the age of 62. It's amazing what you can do.

Although I must admit that when I started rodeoing at age 15 I had no idea that some day I'd intentionally participate in car crashes and slide through flames. Things have a way of evolving that you just can't foresee even a year earlier. I guess that's what enriches your life, along with the people you encounter along the way.

If my stories spark a memory or you'd like to share your experiences, please write to me. This is not the end; my story is ongoing. After you send in your stories, I add the ones I forgot and throw in any new developments, there will be plenty more material to work with. I enjoy a good story as much as the next cowboy and I love to receive mail!

Bear with me as I ramble, diary-style but not necessarily chronologically, through 63 years of dust and sweat and physical danger. This is the story of Buckskin Jack McElrath — so far. The best may be yet to come! For the occasion I dredged up a phrase from my rodeo announcing days: "Hold on! Take a seat! This is one wild ride!

        Jack McElrath
        P.O. Box 103
        Canistota, SD 57012

Diary entry dated June 10, 1948, Sioux Falls, SD:
    Nobody was wearing big felt cowboy hats... except for me. I always wore Levis, boots and my hat. Sometimes I'd ride my bike out to Don Merrill's place, out toward west Sioux Falls from Washington High School or from my folks' house near McKennan Park. During each trip somebody would yell, "Hi, yo Silver! Cowboy, get a horse!"
    So I finally resorted to putting my big green American cowboy hat in a large paper sack and carrying it, dangling from my handle bars, all the way to Don's country place where I kept my horse. Then I could safely put on my hat and be transformed into a cowboy.

This is a true story.

Chapter 1
Back to the Beginning

I've wanted to be a cowboy for as long as I can remember. I spent my formative years on the farm near Moville, IA. My parents, Clyde and Ruth, lived there for many years with the four of us: my brother Neil and sisters Doris and Janice. I was the youngest.

My parents were the salt of the earth. Dad was called "Pete" and later, when he handled the sheep department for Steele-Simon & Co. at the Sioux Falls Stockyards, had the respect of sheep farmers throughout the area. Mom was a great housekeeper and cook. She did her best to make something out of me, but she didn't have much luck!

We had 160 acres of good Iowa farm land in the 1940s, which back then went for about $100 an acre but today would fetch over $2,000. My earliest memory is playing with my little red wagon. When I was about three years old, I saw some fellows working on the road near our place. I went over to talk to them. They told me they needed some big rocks to put in a hole and asked me if I would like to go get them in my wagon. I worked hard, hurrying as fast as I could. I struggled with the big boulders and when I finally reached the road with my load, the men were gone. It was my first disappointment.

Life on the land can be rough. It's hard work and a constant struggle to live in sync with the elements. For a while we lived on a farm a couple miles north of Oto, a very small town in western Iowa. The big old farm house made spooky noises. The windows rattled when the wind blew. One of my jobs was to fetch wood from the wood shed, carrying it in for the heater in the living room and the stove in the kitchen. Making those trips in the dark, listening to the noises, is a frightening memory.

The weather was always a challenge and sometimes snowstorms moved in as permanent tenants before we finished harvesting. One snowstorm hit on Nov. 11, piling up snowdrifts immediately. I shared a room with my brother, Neil, and the next morning our bedroom was full of snow. We'd only left the window open an inch. I told Neil we had snow all over the room and on the bed. He said I must be dreaming. It seemed remarkably real when I stepped out of bed barefoot into the snow, slipped on the stairway and fell down the stairs. When Mom opened the door at the bottom of the stairs, I rolled out. But the adventure wasn't over yet. We still had to shovel snow to get to the outhouse. It sure was cold taking down your britches in the outhouse during the winter!

One of my favorite activities was riding my pony. His name was Topsey. I had a cart for Topsey and each fall I'd hook him up to the cart and go down to the big, flat bottomland to pick corn. Once I hit a bump and the bang board hit me, knocking me off the cart and breaking my nose.

Despite the pitfalls, I loved the farm and always enjoyed farmwork over the years. I worked like a man until I was nine, even driving a team of mules and a tractor. One of my jobs was to stack hay loose in the field. Walking in a haystack, forking and packing it, was one of the hottest jobs around. Most of our feed went to fattening our cattle for market. We also raised hogs, cows and chickens.

I also helped Dad put hay in the hayloft. This was done by putting slings under the haystack in the wagon. The wagon was positioned on one end of the barn. A rope ran from a team of horses, across the top of the loft and down and out the other side of the barn to the slings to pull the hay up the side and into the huge door of the hayloft.

Once the big grey team of horses got spooked. They

backed over the doubletrees — the wood or metal device hooked to the tugs to form the harness —and when they moved ahead it came up and scared them. They took off and I couldn't stop them. They pulled the rope completely through the barn and to the other end of the farm. I was afraid to go around the barn to see if Dad had survived. He was OK, but upset.

There were plenty of daredevil stunts to pull on the farm. Sometimes I climbed 60 feet to the top of the windmill and hung upside down. There was always something to do with my collie dog Rusty and, later, my pinto pony named Bird. Then my parents sold the farm. Dad went to work at the Sioux City, IA, stockyards for a year in the 1940s. It was a troubled time for me. The switch put me behind in school so I had to stay in during recess. Living in town, going to a city school and without a horse or dog or friends made me miserable. Then my dad transferred to Sioux Falls and worked at the stockyards for 20 years.

As they say, you can take the boy out of the country, but you can't take the country out of the boy. This is how I came to be riding my bike all over town with my cowboy hat in a paper bag. But I persevered, seeking out saddle club and junior horseman friends and determined to test my skills in the rodeo.

I couldn't see where my cowboy skills would lead me back in 1948, when I first tried my hand at at bulls Ben Brune's Flying B Stables on 33rd and Euclid Avenue. Neither could my parents, but they always encouraged me to try my best at whatever I did. They may have been happier with the way my siblings turned out. My brother Neil is a good businessman. He's in his early 70s now, with nine children and a good wife.

Neil didn't want to hang around rural Iowa, so he headed off to the Navy and then to California. He was always interested in fashion and got into top management at

Bullocks Department Store in Los Angeles, then opened his own up-scale stores called Neil's Apparel throughout the desert Southwest.

My sisters Janice and Doris also did well. Doris and her husband Vince O'Connell stayed close to the farm and now, retired and in their mid-70s, have a beautiful hillside home overlooking the Little Sioux River Valley. They and their three children enjoy a healthy Iowa farm life.

The O'Connells are snowbirds, spending time in Las Vegas in the winter. My sister Janice and her husband Ralph are longtime Las Vegas residents. They made it big time in the office management field, handling health and welfare plans for the union trades during the good times of the '60s. We did a lot of things together over the years and I'm happy to see them play golf and enjoy their new home right up on the mountainside. They can look out over the valley and watch the Las Vegas light show each night.

It seems that we're a family of Vegas-lovers. My parents spent their retirement years splitting their time between the Midwest and Las Vegas. Dad died in 1978 and Mom in 1991.

I never want to lose touch with my roots back in South Dakota and have chosen to live here for the time being. However, it never fails to thrill me to set foot back on the Strip.

Diary entry dated July 12, 1949, Ft. Pierre, SD

Casey Tibbs, who later became my friend, won his first world saddle bronc title this year. He went on to win six saddle bronc riding championships and was one of my heroes. He managed to put South Dakota cowboys on the map, and helped so many of us out along the way. In fact, I see Casey's athletic prowess as deserving of a TV movie as any of the so-called sports heroes of today.

Chapter 2
The Rodeo Years

I can trace all of my stunt-filled life back to 1948. That's when I got my first taste of rodeoing and I've been hungry for that first appetizer of danger, excitement and travel. Nowadays they teach you how to ride saddle broncs, bulls and bulldogging steers at schools, but back then you learned by doing. I fine-tuned my methods, practicing at rodeos across the country for nearly 40 years. I'd like to share some of what I learned, sometimes at the hands of masters like Casey Tibbs, but mostly by trying to hang on to some mighty fierce critters who were as much contestants as I was.

My first saddle bronc was a big horse called Strip. This virgin ride took place at Ben Brune's rodeo arena at the corner of 33rd & Euclid in Sioux Falls when I was 15. Saddle bronc riding is an eight-second contest and I managed to make it to the whistle on my first ride.

Equipment, as with any sport, is very important. The saddle used in this event is the same type for each contestant. It's very important to have your own saddle and set the stirrups to fit you. I always tied mine far forward so I could spur forward free and easy. And the bind on my stirrup leather always felt firm as I gripped the front swells of the saddle just above my knees. I can't remember how much my first saddle cost, but today they're well over $1,000 for a good one. I set my saddle far forward on the horse, nice and snug, and the back cinch went way back to my horse's flank.

I used a halter, of course, and furnished a bronc rein which is a loose braided rope about six feet long. I used powdered rosin between my leather chaps so they didn't slip over the front of the saddle.

I never used a glove on my riding hand because I wanted to feel the rein (I ran the rein between my little finger and ring finger). My other hand was up in the air because contestants can't touch the horse or saddle with their free hand. The hold on the rein is vital. An average hold is about six inches in back of your saddle's front.

Spurs go over the point of the horse's shoulder and your toes turn out when the horse's hooves hit the ground during the first jump out of the chute. Two judges are watching this closely, scoring your spurring action front to back on each jump. They score you and your horse from 1-25 with a total of 100 as perfect. A good bronc rider will score 70-80.

You can't learn to ride a bronc from reading a book, and there are quite a few schools springing up. You have to get on a lot of horses to learn how it's done. I'd say I rode about 500 horses in the 40 years I was in the arena.

There were some good horses among these 500, including Cloudy Day of Barnes' Rodeo, Major Reno of the Potter Rodeo, Nylon of the Steiner Rodeo Co., Sheep Mountain of the Sutton Rodeo Co., Why Cry, Turkey Track and Strip of Ben Brune's stock.

I won sometimes, even when contesting against the best like Casey Tibbs and Dennis Reiners. It was on a bronc called Headlight at the Sioux Falls Fair and Rodeo one year when I scored more than Casey. Because the horses are all drawn, it helps to draw a good one you can ride for a win.

When the eight seconds is up, two pickup men ride in to pick you up. You hand your rein to the man on your rein side and then get over and off in back of him. Try to get down on the side away from your horse to avoid getting kicked. Some bronc riders can kick free and land on their feet well away from the bronc. But this requires a special talent and isn't for everyone. Monty Henson was the best I've ever seen at this.

Saddle bronc riding can be great fun when you and your horse are in sync. I'd still like to ride and haven't entirely given up the notion that I might saddle up again!

Bulls, unlike saddle broncs, are tricky characters. No one rides every bull they get on; in fact, if you rode half of them you'd be doing great. I first eased down on a bull back in 1948 at Ben Brune's arena.

The bull, named Tarzan, was big and white with long horns. The bull riding contest is for eight seconds. I managed to hang on to Tarzan for six seconds. My last bull ride occurred 38 years later at the Old Timers Rodeo held at Horseman's Park in Las Vegas. In between I probably got on 500 bulls, some of them really good stock from Barnes, Korkow, Sutton, Tibbs and Potter rodeo companies.

Bull riding is dangerous. There is a braided bull rope that loops around the bull, which is pulled snug, and then around your hand. You slip on a glove and rosin the bull rope, which you grip, fingers forward, in a flat, braided handhold. I rode with my right hand, leaving my left hand free for balance. Touching anything with the free hand disqualifies a rider.

You furnish your own bull rope. The grip in your hand holds the rope on the bull. A cowbell strapped onto the rope helps disengage the rope when you pull off and the ringing adds to the excitement of the event. I locked my bull spur rowels to help get ahold of the bull, with my toes turned out. All bull riders do.

Between holding on with one hand and my spurs, my free hand in the air, my chin down, my chest out, my body back, my eyes on the bull's hump and moving with the bull's contortions, it's a mighty long eight seconds!

Getting off is very important. You pull your hand free, pull your leg up and over the bull as you turn away from him and towards your riding hand. I always tried to land on my feet, scrambling away from the bull. Clowns will help get the bull's attention away from you.

Because the bull you get is the luck of the draw, you always hope you get a good one. Judges score the bull's performance from 1 to 25 and your ride from 1 to 25. A perfect ride would score 100, but a good ride usually gets a 75-85.

I scored in the 80s a few times, once winning the event at the Sioux Empire Fair and Rodeo the year Casey Tibbs produced the rodeo. That was back in the early 1960s when I drew a good black Angus bull who spun very fast. I also won bull riding events throughout Iowa, Minnesota, Wisconsin, South Dakota, North Dakota and even a few down in Louisiana.

I didn't miss a chance at steer wrestling — also called bulldogging — either. This event features two men on horseback who approach on either side of a running steer. The hazer keeps the steer running straight while the steer wrestler gets off his horse, takes hold of the steer's horns to stop him and then throws him down.

We began by backing our horses into the box on each side of the steer chute. The steer has a rope around his neck, held together by a string. Another rope is under spring tension and across in front of your horse. When the steer leaves the chute, the rope on the steer pulls a pin, releasing the rope in front of your horse. This rope is held together with a string and if you start too soon, you break the string and 10 seconds is added to your time.

I always backed my horse as far back in the box as I could. I held the saddle horn with my left hand because a quarter horse goes right out from under you if you don't hold on! I set my left stirrup a bit shorter than the right. This helped me get down fast. I either called or nodded my head to the man opening the steer gate when I was ready.

I timed my dismount for when I could reach over the steer's back. I started at the tail and let my horse carry my feet out front. My left hand came down on top of the steer's left hand and my right arm hooked the right horn on the inside of my elbow. I pushed down with my left hand, turning my body to the left. When the steer's nose came up, I reached it with my left hand and lay the steer down.

When the steer's head and legs are all out straight the field judge drops his flag. The timers "2" punch their stop watches and you have your time. My fastest run was 3.2 seconds at an R.C.A. Barnes' Rodeo at Kasson, MN, in 1960. The winning run in Sioux Falls in 1969 was 3.7. Don Merrill was around 3 seconds at the Sioux Falls Rodeo once, but any run around 5 seconds is good and will win some rodeos.

A lot of the timing depends on the steer's size and head start. They average around 500 pounds, but can easily go up to 700 pounds. Steers are only used for one season. Your steer is the luck of the draw and obviously some are better to handle than others.

I really enjoyed steer wrestling and usually did quite well. I had a great quarter horse called "Ike Bailey" in 1959-61 and Don Merrill and I won a lot with him.

It was short excursion from the chute to the microphone. In fact, I first worked the mike as a teenager. Our junior horseman club produced a number of events and I found myself behind the mike many times. I announced for the Ben Brune Rodeo Co. and later for the Bob Barnes' Rodeo Co. I remember in 1963 at the rodeo in Buffalo, MN, when Ditman Mitchell, the regular announcer, handed me the mike and said, "Handle the saddle bronc riding for a while." I managed to put out a lot of cowboy information. It was just so natural to talk about your friends and fellow contestants. Lots of fans came up after the rodeo and told me they appreciated the information.

The rodeo secretary furnishes announcers with a program which lists the events, contestants, special acts, necessary introductions, names of sponsors and local information. Outside of that, it's up to you to keep it interesting and fast-paced. It wasn't difficult for me to ad lib because I had so many stories about the stock, cowboys and cowgirls that I was never at a loss for words. I know one thing: it's hard to have a good rodeo without a good announcer, and it's a waste to have a good announcer without a good sound system.

I worked with Donita Barnes at many rodeos in the 1960s. She was the secretary and one of the timers. She helped out a lot and when I had to ride, she'd fill in on the microphone. She was really busy at the Nashua, IA, rodeo one year because I rode a saddle bronc, bulldogged a steer, rode a bull and worked the Flying Buckskins!

Much as I liked announcing, I'll have to bow to some of the all-time greats. Cy Tallon announced the Denver Rodeo for years. With his deep voice, he was probably one of the best rodeo announcers of his time. Clem McSpadden added as much professional information as anyone. And Chip Morris announced many Midwest rodeos in the '40s and '50s. He started every rodeo in this melodramatic way: "From the rock-bound coast of New England to the sandy beaches of California, from the snow-capped peaks of Old Calgary to the burning deserts of Nevada and Arizona, cowboys and cowgirls gather together to contest for the prize money put up by your local sponsor."

It seemed like a natural progression to move on to announcing and later to producing rodeos and fairs and from there, to develop and perform stunts. I reveled in the action, whether it was oat-powered or gasoline-powered!

Above, left: Ruth McElrath and 8-month-old Jack pose on the homestead farm north of Moville, IA, in 1934.

Above, right: Jack built this soapbox derby car, Hellcat, when he was 13. Jack was living in Sioux Falls, SD, at the time. Jack spent $2.30 to build the car, which broke down during the race.

Above, left: Jack and his niece Pat Bradshaw sit astride Jack's horse Bird in 1942 near Moville.

Above right: Jack sits proudly on the front steps of the family's home in Moville.
From Jack's private collection

Billboards in the Los Angeles area advertise Neil McElrath's clothing stores. Neil's daughter Meg, Jack's niece, is pictured on the billboard.
From Jack's private collection

Jack and his dad Clyde "Pete" McElrath were dressed in their Sunday best, Sioux Falls, SD, in 1945.
From Jack's private collection

Above right: Jack always love the snow and still does. This photo was taken in Iowa in January and is one of the few which doesn't show Jack on a horse. (It was too cold for the horse!)
From Jack's private collection

Right: Jack couldn't be parted from his big green cowboy hat. He often put in a brown paper sack when he rode his bike across town to Don Merrill's place to ride his horse.

Below: Jack and his cousin Bob Logan grew up together in Moville. Bob still lives in Moville.
From Jack's private collection

The McElrath children and their mother gathered at Janice's home in Las Vegas in 1989. From left: Doris, Jack, Ruth, Janice and Neil. Jack's Dad died in 1978 and his mother passed away in 1991. Jack's parents are buried at Moville.

From Jack's private collection

Clair Dunkelberger's dad drove this wagon for Lakeside Dairy in Sioux Falls, SD.

Left: Jack and Janice take in a show at the Folies Bergere at the famed Las Vegas night spot, the Tropicana Hotel, in 1961. Jack was a bit taken aback by nude showgirls, but quickly recovered to enjoy the show.

Left: Doris and Vince O'Connell live in Oto, IA, where they built a new home overlooking the Little Sioux River valley.
Below: The McElrath's home on Carter Place.

The whole McElrath clan enjoys a few moments of laughter in Janice's new home in 1997. From left: Ralph Long, David Barnhill (Jack's nephew), Neil, Janice, Doris, Jack and Vince. *All photos from Jack's private collection*

Left: Janice, Jack and Doris take a ride at the old homestead farm north of Moville in 1935.

Below: Jack's class reunion met in Sioux Falls in June, 1992.

Jack announces at the huge National Dairy Cattle Congress and Rodeo at Waterloo, IA, produced by Barnes PRCA Rodeo. To Jack's right is Donita Barnes, rodeo secretary. In front of the chutes, on left, are two of Jack's friends: saddle bronc rider Harold Allman from Ft. Pierre, SD, and bronc rider Kenny Carlson from Alden, MN. This rodeo included five performances, a real test of Jack's vocal stamina.

All photos from Jack's private collection

Rip the Dog, Dian Daly the Follies Showgirl, John John the Pony and Jack the Clown mess around in Las Vegas in 1975.
Photo courtesy of Ken Jones

Jack works to develop a new stunt on the El Dorado Dry Lake Bed outside Las Vegas. Jack hangs on a wire strung between two pickups in 1973.
Photo from Jack's Private Collection

Jack stands on his head on the patient Highlander named Scotty. This was part of Jack's show at Underwood, ND, in 1975. The show included Dee Dee Ortman, singer Lola Jean Dillon, stuntman Jim Devlin and clown John Guertin.

All photos from Jack's private collection

Jack was in Elko, NV, for the Oldtimers Rodeo Association, now called the National Senior Pro Rodeo Association. Jack was picking up some points in the saddle bronc event in 1985.

Jack and the Flying Buckskins performed at hundreds of rodeos and fairs across the country from 1965 through 1976. Jack rode on the backs of Buck, left, Champ, middle, and Bob, right. This performance was in Sibley, IA, in 1975. The Buckskins were registered Quarterhorses.

Above: Jack in his beloved cowboy hat, circa 1964. Right: Jack is about drop into a water tank from a 60-foot tower at the South Dakota State Fair in 1977. This act was featured in Jack's shows throughout Canada and the United State in 1977 and 1978.

Above, left: Jack competes in the National Senior Pro Rodeo Association saddle bronc event at Horseman's Park in Las Vegas in 1985. Just behind Jack's horse, which was from the Swanney Kirby Rodeo stock, is Dennis Reiners, 1970 World's Champ PRCA saddle bronc rider. **Above right:** Jack featured the chain spin and bullwhip act at numerous malls in 1984. *All photos from Jack's private collection*

Jack sits with Scotty, the trained Highlander bull, as he discusses the skydogging stunt with pilot Cliff Foss in 1972 near Canistota, SD.

Jack goes on to demonstrate how to take hold of a steer and lay him down.

Cliff drops Jack into excellent position above the steer during the Canistota Sports Day in 1972. The run itself wasn't quite so successful, but viewers across the country got to watch the newsworthy attempt, via CBS.

Jack stands on Scotty and takes aim with a bow and arrow at balloon targets held by wife Karen. This act was staged in Walla Walla, WA, in 1970 as a benefit performance for the Veterans Hospital.
All photos from Jack's private collection

Charlie Brown goes for a ride on Tuffy. Neither one is frightened by the scruffy looking clown. Jack was the clown and bullfighter at the Crooks, SD, High School Rodeo in 1970. The following year Jack moved up, announcing for the rodeo, which featured Sutton Rodeo stock.

Pet chihuahua Tiki and Jack take a rest at Mesquite, NV, in 1983. They were headed home to Las Vegas after being out on tour.

Jack and Rip pause before the show at Underwood, ND. Jack worked with Rip on security duty in Las Vegas during the winter and took Rip on tour during the summer. Rip always brought a roar from the crowd when he chased the clown up on top of the truck, in the meantime taking a bite out of the clown's britches.

All photos from Jack's private collection

Jack prepares for the next tour with this publicity photo, taken in the backyard of his Las Vegas home in 1983.
Photo from Jack's private collection

Thanks to Jeri Cunningham, Jack was involved in many Western mall promotions. This shot, which features Westy the Panda the Western Mall mascot and Jack's secretary, Mrs. Anthony.

Photo courtesy of the Argus Leader

Above: Jack in Sam's Town Hotel and Casino in Las Vegas in 1982.
Right: Jack practices his trick roping with wife Sylvia in the backyard of their Las Vegas home.
Photos from Jack's private collection

Jack and Bob perform at the National Orange Show and Rodeo at San Bernardino, CA, in 1970. Flying U provided the stock at the rodeo. Jack received a trophy plaque from the show committee, identical to the one presented to Roy Rogers during his heyday.
Photo courtesy of Faine Photos

Jack was decked out in his war bonnet during this roman ride at the Sitting Bull Stampede in Mobridge, SD, in July 1970. With Sutton rodeo stock, the rodeo was always a popular event in northern South Dakota.
Photo from Jack's private collection

Jack checks his roman riding equipment prior to a promotion show at the Western Mall in 1970.

One of Jack's stunt cars is parked in the driveway of his Las Vegas home. The Western Casino was one of Jack's boosters.

Jack stands in front of a typical promotion signs in Illinois, inviting fans to witness Jack's record jumps in 1988.

Artist Ray Kelly used this photo, taken in 1988 at Cadillac, MI, for the collage on the cover of *The Cowboy Stuntman*. Photos from Jack's private collection

Jack and Jerry Olson work with Jerry's buffalo in Denver, CO, at the stock show. One of Jack's greatest regrets was that he couldn't afford to buy Jerry's buffalo, rig and equipment for $20,000 in 1966. Jack believes the offer, which was made by Jerry's father LaRue, would have set him up for life.

The Sioux Falls Arena was the site of many of Jack's exploits. He even helped build the facility.

Above left: Jack's trailer promotes the 1969 Flying Bucksin Rodeo, all over the Midwest throughout the summer. Bob Gartner made sure Jack had a good Hale horse trailer.
Above right: Souvenir ticket for the Thrill Show was quite a bargain!

Jack rides Bob in the center of the Sioux Falls Arena during the introductions. The concrete floor was covered b a foot of clay, sand and straw. Jack produced the rodeo from 1969-1972.

Jack goes air borne in the most unbelievable motorcycle jump imaginable. The feat brought tears and fears from the audience, along with an audible gasp as Jack landed on dozens of cardboard boxes.

At the Sioux Falls Arena

Right: Just before he took his masterful motorcycle leap at the Sioux Falls Arena Thrill Show in 1976, Jack said good-bye to his loyal fans. Jack had been listening to Evil Knievel in Las Vegas before his jumps and decided to adopt the same style at the Sioux Falls show. Bob Kunkel, the Arena manager, broadcast on KXRB that the jump was impossible.
Below: Karen McElrath takes Shag the Highlander, the first bull Jack trained, for a jump over the moon at the Arena in 1970.
All photos from Jack's private collection

At the Houston Astrodome

Being the featured stuntman at the Houston Astrodome in front of 50,000 is as good as it gets. Gary Beall was driving the car; Jack was doing the carefully timed leaping. First, Jack was hoisted to the top of the car with a crane, then the camera caught the action as Jack jumped ahead of the crash. The publicity surrounding this stunt was the equivalent of winning an academy award and ensured easy bookings at county fairs.

Above, left: Jack quickly departs a wooden pedestal as a car driven by Gary Beall crashes into it at Isanti, MN. Gary's dad Bill Beall, who passed away in 1997, stands in the foreground. Above, right: Jack did 18 stunts during three shows on a single day at Jackson, MI, a total unlikely to be surpassed any time soon. Who would want to?
Photos from Jack's private collection

National Enquirer

Jack McElrath readies for the jump. — FLAMES engulf car and almost catch the daredevil.

DEVIL SURVIVES SUICIDE STUNT

WEARING NO protective clothing except for a helmet, leather jacket, and gloves, Hollywood daredevil stuntman Jack McElrath perched atop a car packed with hay and gasoline, ready to leap an instant before it exploded into flame.

The timing had to be precise. Jack was to dive from the car exactly one quarter of a second — no more, no less — before the gasoline was ignited.

He waited a split second too long, however, and the car erupted into flame before he could get clear of it.

Luckily, he was hurled from the flaming pyre by a hidden ejection device, soared high above the raging inferno, hung there for an agonizing moment, and then plunged through the flames to make a three-point landing atop the roof of another car.

Jack walked away smiling and happy to have survived.

Trumpets Stunts

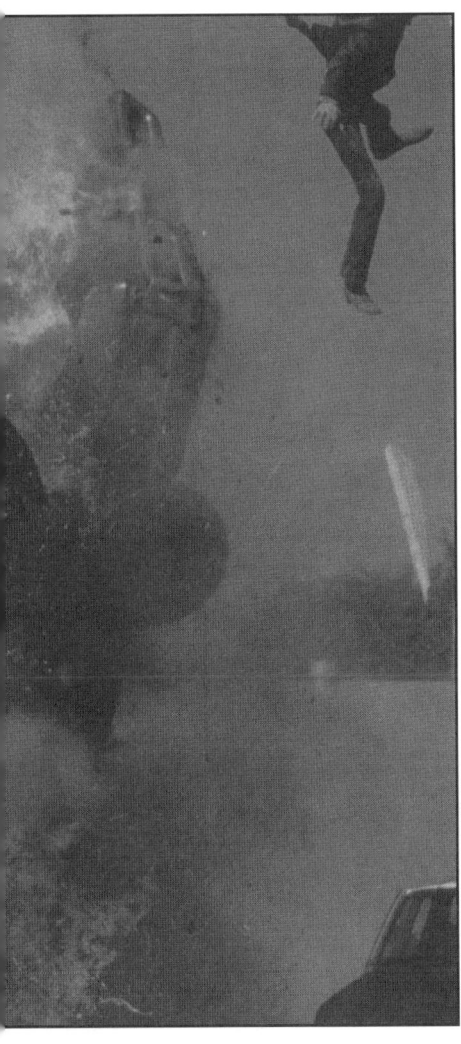

Jack's stunts have brought him attention from many media, including that famed tabloid, the *National Enquirer*.

The Enquirer's photographer, Bob Warner, took this series of photos at the Steel County Fair in Owatonna, MN, in 1985. This was the first time that Jack did the leap from the stop of the Steel Wall Auto, but went on to perform this stunt many more times, including the stint at the Houston Astrodome and the South Dakota State Fair.

Gilbert Slemin also performed this feat at the South Dakota State Fair, and Jack, in a role reversal, drove the car. That was a test of Jack's stuntman skills! Jack says that when the car hits the steel wall, it sounds like a caterpillar tractor dropping off a cliff into a junkyard full of cars.

This sensational stunt was used as the show's finale, an untoppable visual feast for spectators.

Above, left: Hunter, ND, on a hot, windy summer day in 1976 was the site of Jack's sensational leap over the trailer with clown John Guertin lying on top. Jack and his Yamaha 250 sailed over the trailer, the truck and into the boxes. Jim Devlin and Dee Dee Ortman are holding the boxes against the wind.
Above right: Jack and his dune buggy crash the firewall at Spencer, IA, in 1991. Amazingly, nobody was hurt.

Above: Jack emerges from the fire tunnel at a fair near Beaver, UT, in 1983.
Right: Gilbert Slemin jumps his motorcycle over the spinning rotors of a helicopter at the South Dakota State Fair in 1988.
All photos from Jack's private collection

Left: How truly amazing that Bob the Wonder Horse and Heidi the Wonder Dog could overcome their natural fear of height, obeying Jack's commands.

Below: General Lee, automotive star of the *Dukes of Hazzard* TV show, appeared with Jack in Savannah, MO, in 1988.

From left: Dusty Lee Rivers, Liz Olsen and Jack practice a new stunt at their Las Vegas practice arena in 1973. John Guertin is driving.

Below: The stunt show crew, all fancied up in their Wrangler shirts and Wrangler jeans, say thanks to their benefactor in East Berlin, IL, in 1986.
Photos from Jack's private collection

Jack and his trusty dune buggy perform the ever-popular firewall crash in Evanston, WY, in 1992.
All photos from Jack's private collection

This shot was taken just a few seconds earlier and from the other side of the firewall crash at the Evanston Rodeo Grounds.

Above, right: Gale Anderson watches as the car used in the steel wall crash is raised into position. Gale was an excellent engineer on positioning the car at St. Peter, MN, in 1988.
Above, left: The steel wall stays upright in a 70-mph wind at Williston, ND, in 1988.

Jack thrilled the crowd with this stunt in Hastings, NE. Jack was totally engulfed in fire and flames and lucky to get out alive. The problem was that the dune buggy's engine cut out as it hit the ramp.

All photos from Jack's private collection

Jack still had the right stuff during the National Seniors Pro Rodeo in Elko, NV, in 1985. He stayed on bronc Sheep Mountain for 8 seconds, a successful ride.

Diary entry dated June 10, 1952, Clear Lake, SD

I joined the Rodeo Cowboys Association in 1952 and officially became Number 2212. Clear Lake was a Professional Rodeo Cowboys Association (PRCA) rodeo and I wanted to ride bulls. I rode two bulls and won $45. Since the entry fee was $10, I cleared $35! It was a big deal. Don Merrill and I were in the wild cow milking contest and also won a few dollars there.

There were lots of rodeos in 1952 and I even traveled as far as Texas and Louisiana that fall. I wanted to rodeo full time, but there was no way to make money at it. In fact, I was lucky to make enough to cover my expenses. I made lots of friends and was never lonely.

Chapter 3
The Military Doesn't Put Up With Many Stunts

Rather than get drafted into the Army, I grudgingly signed up for the Air Force. I was sent to Parks A.F.B. at Hayward, CA, where I enjoyed my 12 weeks of playing G.I. Joe ... otherwise known as Basic Training. I wanted to be the very best airman and I did very well at basic, except for the one time when I folded a blanket wrong.

Even though my interests ran more toward security or operating heavy equipment, the Air Force decided that I would spend my four-year career working on jet fighters. So I caught a ride in an old C-46 to Amarillo, TX, for 16 more weeks of school.

Now I've never had much patience with sitting around and that's exactly what jet fighter school was all about. My six-hour day began at 6 a.m. in the classroom and wrapped up at noon, still in the classroom. I had always been active and with 18 hours of free time staring me in the face, I grappled with what to do. At first I walked around and around the base. I read books, rode the bus back and forth to town. But this was back in 1953 and we were warned to stay away from rough or minority sections of Amarillo.

And then it was June and rodeo blood began pumping hotly through my veins. I wanted to be back in my old stomping grounds, following the rodeos through Minnesota, South Dakota and Iowa. I hadn't wanted this Air Force "deal" anyway. So there I was. My accumulated pay of $72 a month was burning a hole in my pocket and rodeo fever was burning a hole in my brain.

One weekend I bought a ticket to Rapid City and hopped a bus in Amarillo. I thrilled to the thought of riding it all the way to the Black Hills but in my heart knew I'd reluctantly get off somewhere up the line and turn around again. Somehow my heart and my brain lost communication and I just kept going!

Once I hit town I met some of my high school buddies — Ken Carlson and Don Merrill — who had been contesting at the high school rodeo in Rapid City. They gave me a ride back to eastern South Dakota where I picked up the reins of Midwestern rodeo action as naturally as I put on a pair of blue jeans. I wondered if they missed me back in Amarillo, but these thoughts were pushed to the back of my mind as I concentrated on animals rather than airplanes.

It quickly came to the forefront, however, one day when the county sheriff showed up at a rodeo and asked my friends if they'd seen me. And faster than a timed ride on a bucking bronc, I arrived at this conclusion: I'd better get back to Amarillo before the law did it for me!

My parents — who had gotten a call about my AWOL status and were mighty worried — suggested that I drive their 1950 Buick back to the base. This shows my dad's sharp perception. He knew that having a car around would cut my boredom and reinforce my waning feeling of freedom. My mom rode along on the drive south and took the bus back. The Air Force had quite a homecoming reception for me. The air police made out like I was a real big-time outlaw, meeting me with guns and spotlights and handcuffs. I spent two days and two nights in the lock-up, plenty of time to decide that I *could* and *would* be a good, law-abiding airman. All young people should experience being locked up. It really helps clarify things and believe me, it kept me clear for a lifetime!

The officer in charge of the stockade made a visit one Saturday morning. I was the first guy in a long line, anxious to visit with him and repent. He asked if I was ready to get out. YES, SIR! Will you be a good airman? YES, SIR! You will be out this afternoon. THANK YOU, SIR!

I'm here to tell you that I spent the next four years as a good airman. When I completed my course, I was stationed at Travis A.F.B. near Vacaville, CA, where the giant B-36 airplanes dominated the base. They expected me to work on those huge aircraft with a 300-foot wing span and 10 engines. I was assigned to the 72nd Squadron and worked on the flight line, changing spark plugs and oil filters on the 28-piston engines.

Then I spent 90 days on Guam, mostly swimming and driving trucks. Guam is an island about 28 miles long and 8 miles wide. It's surrounded by sandy beaches and high cliffs, some reaching up to 200 or 300 feet in places. Coral reefs surround much of the island and it is really a beautiful sight from the air. Most of the interior of the island was jungle so thick you couldn't walk into it. The air base itself was very modern in every respect. The runway was paved and about two miles long. It went right over one of the cliffs, making it possible for a plane to drop off the end of the runway into the ocean. It was interesting to see the old Japanese air base, tanks and bunkers left over from World War II. Must have been one hell of a battle on those islands!

Despite the fact that I was supposed to be tending to wounded airplanes, my favorite time was spent at Travis A.F.B. where I got to develop the horse stables for Special Services. The following fall I fell into a good deal at the base. They wanted to set up stables and I got wind of it and managed to get assigned to the project. I promptly came up with a plan to drag some surplus crew shacks off the base to 300 acres just outside the main gate. These old shacks were only 10 feet wide by 16 feet long and had been left on the air strip. When I went down to see the officers and asked if they wanted the shacks removed, they replied that they sure did.

So the next day I went to the motor pool and signed

out a huge Coleman tug tractor. I drove down to the air strip, hooked up one of the shacks and dragged it through camp to the side gate. The guard on duty stopped me and asked where I was going with the shack. I told him I was taking it out to the stables. He asked where the stables were located because he had never heard about them. He didn't like the situation a bit. Here I was with a tractor and shack and no authorization permit. After turning it over in his mind, including the fact that I drove all through the camp and nobody stopped me, the guard decided to let me go. Away I went, one shack out, only nine more to go.

As soon as I got off duty the next day, I went down to the motor pool for the tractor and got another shack. Everything went fine until I reached the gate. There was a different guard who didn't buy my story. When he finally realized I had taken one out the previous day with no problem and that there were nine more to be moved, he let me go.

After that I had no trouble. No one reported me. The air strip was cleared of shacks and we had shacks for tack rooms and offices. Everybody was happy. Thenm I moved our trailer out there and purchased the first six rental horses and equipment. We were in business. Within a year we had two 100-foot barracks built, along with a show ring and we stabled about 60 horses. Many of them were owned by airmen and officers.

Even after four years in the Air Force, airplanes just couldn't replace my affection for living, breathing animals. I was anxious to return to civilian life, even if it meant working as a lather for $1.50 an hour in the cold and snow.

Diary entry dated June 20, 1973, Las Vegas, NV

I worked most of a weekend to drop from Darrell Sorenson's Super Cub. This wasn't just a practice run at the event I've come to call skydogging. This time it was being filmed by *Thrillseekers*, the TV show hosted by Chuck Connors. I made many runs to get enough film for the half-hour show, both downtown and at the Las Vegas strip. It was an exhausting yet exhilarating day in the dry lake bed and I could see that this stunt would be a big crowd pleaser in the years to come. The dare to try skydogging, believe it or not, came from a radio program.

Chapter 4
Skydogging Isn't As Easy As It Looks

Denny Oviatt was the 6 a.m. KSOO radio personality in Sioux Falls in the late 1960s. I used to drive in from Canistota, SD, and spend some time on the air with Denny. This was an easy 30-mile drive from my 10-acre place back in the late '60s and early '70s. I was working at Ben-Hur Ford at the time and getting air time really moved those cars!

Anyhow, one morning Denny and I were talking about bulldogging a steer from an airplane. I originally got the idea from Milt Hinkel, an old man I met at a rodeo in Wisconsin. He told me about how he hired a Mexican to jump from a low-flying plane down in Old Mexico in the 1920s. Thousands of people showed up to watch, but nobody showed up to jump. The crowd threatened to shoot Milt if he didn't perform the stunt, so Milt went ahead. He landed in the rocks and got all busted up, but at least they didn't kill him!

Denny urged me to try the dangerous stunt, and for some reason I agreed. It was always a rush to me to figure out what would appeal to a crowd and then try a new stunt. Most of my stunts were not only dangerous, but designed for crowd appeal.

My friend Cliff Foss (brother of World War II legend and former South Dakota Governor Joe Foss) farmed east of Sioux Falls and he had a Piper Super Cub airplane. So one cold winter morning the two of us flew low over the fields and I hung out the side. I was trying to get a feel for the stunt and thinking maybe we could do this.

By May of 1972 I had found a suitable spot to try the

stunt and we were practicing at Ortman's landing strip in Canistota. Cliff flew about 12 feet above a hay wagon which Ray Kelly was pulling at about 40 m.p.h. I dropped from the Super Cub into the wagon full of hay. That worked very well. Gale Anderson, Don Merrill and Ray were just as interested in getting the stunt right as Denny and I were.

Finally, we thought we were ready to practice with a running steer. It turned into a wild event when the steer jumped the fence and bolted into the corn field next to the air strip. But we didn't let that small setback deter us. We went ahead and scheduled our first airborne steer wrestling stunt during Canistota's annual Sportsday in July.

A good crowd was on the sidelines, excited about seeing the first-ever skydogging event. Even the CBS *Morning News* showed up to film the event. But when we finally got going it was already twilight. I made the much-heralded drop from Cliff's plane ... and missed the steer. I hit the ground hard. Oh, well. This way of life was exciting and I wasn't looking for any guarantees.

I tried again the next June in the dry lake bed south of Las Vegas. Again, the event was being filmed. The TV show *Thrillseekers*, hosted by Chuck Connors of *The Rifleman* fame, was there and rolling. I had responded to an advertisement for unusual stunts and they liked what I was doing.

We worked all day Saturday and Sunday morning to get the event on film. I had some sensational misses. One run, though, was perfect. I slid in beside the steer, reached over and put the hold on him. To my chagrin, however, the *Thrillseekers* crew was more interested in filming my failures, flips and flops than my successes. I guess it made for a more exciting show to see my bumps and bruises.

Diary entry dated July 28, 1985, Rapid City, SD

I was producing a stunt show at a rodeo arena south of town. Gary Beall had joined the show from Santa Fe, Texas, just south of Houston and this was a whole new area for him.

My wife Sylvia was working the show because she was on vacation from her job at the Western Hotel and Casino is Las Vegas. She was a great addition to the show and it was fun to have her be part of it.

Gary did a feature stunt called The Steel Wall Crash, where we propped up a junkyard auto on its back end with 2x4s holding it upright. Then Gary set it on fire and crashed into the trunk at 60 miles per hour. The upright car flew right over the top of the stunt car. It was a really sensational stunt!

Chapter 5
How to Crash a Stunt Car

This is a how-to chapter for all those readers who really enjoy crashing things themselves. Take it from an expert who has crashed 200-300 autos, motorcycles, dune buggies and trucks over 20 years: you need the right equipment.

Start with an old full-size auto that still runs. Local junk yards are your best bet. Some cars will still get up to 50-60 miles per hour if you do a bit of work on them.

One of my favorites is to speed up a 24-foot-long ramp that's boosted up four feet on the far end. That way I go flying into parked cars about 20-30 feet from the end of the ramp, which I usually built from eight-foot-long 4 x 4s set the long way and two-foot-long 2 x 4s set across. You need six sections to make a 24-foot-long ramp, which is set on pedestals at each section.

Center the car's front tires on each section and make sure the seat belt works. I usually put a big pillow between me and the steering wheel. A good helmet, gloves, jacket and chin guard are all important parts of your uniform.

I used this basic set-up in 1989 in Holly, Michigan. I was driving a 1965 Cadillac that was still in good shape. It had leather seats and spoke wheel rims. This great-looking car made a really spectacular crash auto. I headed up the ramp and head on into the windshield of the "catch" car. Whew, the fans went wild!

I've crashed autos many ways, but Gary Beall and I went on to perfect the Steel Wall Auto Crash. One car is set up on end and propped in place with a couple of 2x4s or

4x4s. If you were seated in the steel wall car you would be looking straight up into the sky. But actually the steel wall auto is empty and you're in your stunt car, racing down the track at 50-60 miles per hour. You crash into the trunk-side of the steel wall, forcing the steel wall auto up over the top of your stunt car. That's if you hit it hard enough and fast enough; if you're slower than 50 mph, it may come down on top of you. I've had this happen plenty of times so now I leave the windows down in case I need to get out in a hurry.

In fact, the time I remember most clearly and maybe the most dangerous moment in my career, happened just this way. I didn't hit the car fast enough and the car fell on top of the car I was driving in Savannah, MO. There I was, engulfed in flames, and needing to make a hasty exit. I calmly concentrated on undoing my seat belt and then leaped out the window. After that stunt, I started carrying a knife. You just never know how reliable Detroit's seat belts might be and I wanted to make sure I wasn't messing around with the buckle while my jeans were on fire!

The most spectacular Steel Wall Auto Crashes happen when you set the car on fire with gas and hay. Having the burning steel wall fall on top of me was not my idea of a good time! Gary Beall and I worked this stunt together a lot during the '80s. In fact, I decided to try standing on top of the steel wall and jumping off into a pile of boxes as Gary hit the steel wall with the stunt car.

We first tried this at the Steel County Fair in Owatonna, MN, in 1985. Dr. Louis Allegeyer, the fair secretary, had booked our stunt for a Sunday afternoon show. The *National Enquirer* was interested in a photo shoot of the stunt, so photographer Jeff Werner of Los Angeles showed up for the stunt.

Gary and I made the centerfold spread of the *Enquirer* in the November 1985 issue with a spectacular series of photos. Jeff captured Buckskin Jack flying off the top of the steel wall auto as flames shot 20 feet in the air. <u>This</u> is the reason they started making film in color!

Because Gary is from Santa Fe, TX, and knows that area well, he booked us into the Houston Astrodome Auto Thrill Show in January 1986. They made a big production out of our stunt, attracting 50,000 fans for Friday and Saturday night performances. They used a big construction crane to set the car on end. Then I rode the big steel ball, dangling from the cable, from the ground up, up, up to the top of the steel wall auto.

If ever I could have suffered a heart attack, standing atop that auto at the Astrodome might have been the time. As I saw the car barreling toward me, my foot sank through the car's grill. I realized that I couldn't get my shoe out in time to jump safely, so I decided instantly that I had to get the shoe off. As calmly as I could, I bent down, untied my shoelace, pulled my foot free and leaped. This is why they developed velcro for sports shoes! When I look closely at photos of the event today, I can clearly see my white tube sock on my right foot. I'm mighty glad that foot is still attached!

There were lots of TV teams there that weekend, getting our stunt on film. I was living in Las Vegas, so I flew in for the show and back out on Sunday. It was a big-time way to do a show.

Many folks have asked me what I'm thinking about as I'm standing on top of an upended auto and another stunt car is racing toward me at 60 m.p.h. Well, that's a pretty easy one to answer. Total concentration is the key. I can't afford to let my thoughts wander. THIS is the deal. I'm focused only on the fast-approaching auto so that I can jump at the right time. Don't be late! Make it right!

Diary entry dated May 12, 1976, Sioux Falls, SD:
 The 1976 stunt show at the Sioux Falls Arena may have been one of the wildest ever. My feature stunt was to jump my Yamaha 250 motorcycle over 10 farm tractors and auto, set side by side, inside the Arena. The problem was that there was no exit after I landed my motorcycle, which would be traveling at about 60 m.p.h. I came up with a solution I thought would work, but Donna Merrill was worried and crying about the stunt. She didn't think I would make it. I wasn't too sure, either!

Chapter 6
Stunts, Stunts & More Stunts

If there was action and adventure, then I wanted to do it, whether it was on the back of an animal or the back of a machine. This quest for thrills led me into the world of motorsports, especially as I got older.

One of the most spectacular stunts involves fire, of course. That seems to rile up a crowd like no other single stunt ingredient. In 1985 I began performing the fireslide. It's fairly simple, but always gets a rise out of the crowd.

I sit in a farm grain shovel and am pulled into the fire by 12-foot chain attached to a stunt auto. I started out with a fairly short run at first and usually Gale Anderson or Gary Beall drove the car. At each performance I added a couple of feet to the slide. As I lengthened my slide, I also added more water to my water-soaked double Levis, Wrangler shirts and jackets. I always used extreme caution and never left anything exposed to the fire. I was burned in the first four or five slides before I got the hang of it. By the time we performed the fireslide at Husets Speedway near Sioux Falls in 1991 for the *Stuntmasters* TV show, I was up to 150 feet.

Over the years I was pulled through the fireslide by everything from monster trucks to farm tractors to pickup trucks, but each slide was a world record and I wanted it done right.

I started by making a 150-foot long strip of hay and soaking it with five gallons of gas. I set the fire with a six-foot torch, running the entire 150-foot length of the hay and back. It was quite a sight, especially at night when the flames are most visible. My longest slide — 200 feet — was in 1996 at Warren, IL.

Before I latched onto the fireslide stunt, I had been concentrating on motorcycle jumps. In 1976 I produced a stunt show at the Sioux Falls Arena. Kyle Evans and his band entertained and announced the event. Gale Anderson and John Guertin were the clowns. Miss South Dakota Gina Campbell and Tanya Sutton did the singing. The feature stunt was Buckskin Jack McElrath, jumping his motorcycle over 10 autos and farm tractors.

Most of my motorcycle stunts were staged outside where there was ample room for the jump and landing. However, this stunt was inside the Arena and no exit room for a fast-moving bike. In fact, there was just enough room for the 36-foot-long ramp, 10 cars and trucks and 60 feet of cardboard boxes where I planned to land.

My run began in the parking lot and continued around the boiler room of the building across the street, into the Arena and up the ramp, which was nine feet high on the far end and 36 feet long. Bob Kunkel and I had run some tests out in the parking lot to see how my Yamaha 250 would feel at 60 m.p.h. My dirt bike didn't have a speedometer and his bike did. It felt fine and so did I.

The run was a good one and I sailed smoothly over every tractor and left a major wheel dent in the final auto, Ray Kelly's Ford Pinto as I came down. My landing wasn't quite so smooth but every bit as exciting as my jump. As my bike headed for the boxes, I flew over the handlebars, flipped three time and landed solo on 100 boxes!

The crew and fans were delighted I made it. Bob Kunkel jumped for joy. Kyle Evans rushed over and picked me up, then jumped up and down. Crew member Dee Dee Ortman even gave me a big hug. The crowd roared. It was good to be alive.

The Associated Press wire service covered the story and most newspapers across the nation carried it the next day. I didn't ignore the popularity of this stunt and went on to perform it about 200 times from 1975-1989.

My longest jump was 152 feet at the county fair in Nelson, NE, in 1976. I jumped horse trailers set end to end there, although I jumped over whatever was handy at the time. Most of the time I simply used my trailer and truck. Over time this stunt expanded a bit. At an indoor auditorium at Minot, ND, in 1976 I jumped over 10 new autos and into boxes. These indoor jumps were unheard of, mostly because there was just no safe place to land. Many of my jumps were into fire walls or 100-foot-long fire tunnels.

I hit the bottom one day in Jackson, MI, in 1988. There were unreasonable expectations — mostly by me — that I could do three performances in one day, and was the featured attraction in 18 of the stunts. Not only did I set up for each of the shows which included the Steel Wall Crash, but I also had to prepare myself mentally for each stunt. By the time I finished the last performance, I didn't know if I had the strength to even stand up. Luckily, the mother of one of the stunt ladies was standing nearby with a thermos of coffee. She poured me a cup of resuscitating coffee and after I'd downed it, I managed to get up and carry on.

A guy by the name of Gilbert Slemin worked my shows in the summers of 1987 and 1988. He jumped his motorcycle over a helicopter with the blade turning! There was another fellow by the name of Doug "9 Toes" Marble who also worked the shows. He crashed his Harley Davidson into 10 firewalls set 15 feet apart. Doug also performed a crash into a car, flipping over the top and landing in boxes. His stunts were spectacular and he, too, was featured on the *Stuntmasters* TV series.

Diary entry dated October 31, 1995, Sioux Falls, SD:

It may seem incongruous that I took up running when I was over 60 years old, but I've always taken really good care of myself. Here I was, back in South Dakota and facing a long, cold winter. Sioux Falls has a lovely bike trail looping around the city and along the Big Sioux River. Part of it runs along the dike, so I started my runs at Sherman Park, running half a mile and walking half a mile early each morning and ignoring snow and cold.

By spring I could run a mile in eight minutes. Then I started running two miles and last month could run four miles in 40 minutes. The competitor in me roped my better sense and I decided to enter the Trick or Treat Trail Run. Halloween or not, I was scared!

The wind was out of the south and it looked like rain. By 11 a.m. the sun was out and 500 runners were lined up. I managed the first mile in nine minutes and ended the four miles with a time of 39:52. Not bad for an old timer, even though the winner cut my time in half! It pays to stay in shape and eat those vegies!

Chapter 7
My Mind Works as Hard as My Body

Over the years I've been toying with what constitutes a super stunt. The airplane skydogging stunt is spectacular and has received great international attention. The problems began with finding the right location, extended to getting a plane and then I still had to pull it off!

That's why I turned to the fireslide, which is easier to stage and perform. Dressed in double pairs of water-soaked denim clothes, welder gloves, boots and head covering, I'd ride a scoop shovel down a long strip of flaming hay. I boosted the distance 2 feet at each show, gradually increasing the distance so I could set a new world record. I've worked this stunt up to a 200-foot-long sensation over the past 10 years and, in time, plan to work it up to 300 feet (which is much more exciting than watching a football receiver dodge tackles as he tries to run the pigskin down a field that's the same length as my fiery ride!). Riding on the shovel adds a lot to the audience's anticipation.

And then there's the Steel Wall Auto Crash, perhaps one of the most awesome stunts of all time. Fans can't ask for a more compelling sight than a fast-moving car crashing into a blazing line of cars standing on end.

The dive bomber is yet another stunt, where one car goes up a ramp and flies over a fire wall and lands on cars. Keeping all of these stunts in mind, I began thinking about a distance jump, ramp to ramp, that surpasses the world record of 232 feet. I've been close to that already and believe that a mid-1980s Pontiac Fiero — which has its engine almost in the center of the car — would balance well without nosing over on a long jump. The down ramp could be flaming cardboard boxes. Hmmm. This sounds interesting, especially if I first go for a record fire slide and then a record-setting auto jump, back to back.

Another idea I've been mulling over is a package for county fairs where local folks can compete for prizes and money. Called the Haystack race, local competitors can get involved by racing their pickup trucks in figure-eights around two haystacks placed 100 feet apart. Combined with a stunt show, I really think the Haystack race will draw big crowds who will have a good time cheering on the people they know.

This is how my mind works, constantly replaying all the stunts I've seen or performed and exercising my own little version of one-up-manship. Coming up with ideas for new stunts or improving upon some I've seen is the way I pass those long, cold South Dakota winters!

Just as professional athletes stay focused on game day, I've always been totally immersed in my stunts on the day I perform. I have to stay busy, and there's always plenty to do. Because set-up is all important, I've always insisted on doing it myself. There's no way I could just sit around and think about the action yet to come, anyway.

Many days I was already tired by stunt time. And after I performed, there was all of the clean up and loading. I got accustomed to long days with setting up, performing, loading up and then spending long nights driving to the next location. Why did I do it? I love it. Always have, always will.

It helps that I handle stress well. I stay relaxed and cool. Many times after a show I'd remain behind to sign posters and photos for fans. That's when a fan would ask, "Hey, man. What are you on to do a stunt like that?" There's a pretty succinct answer to that, maybe even the precursor of today's anti-substance abuse message. **"Nothing. Never."** There's no way you could do what I do when under the influence of anything other than practice, skill and determination.

Which brings up another one of the beliefs I've lived by and would like to pass on. Conditioning is very important. I feel so strongly about this. Walking is great, cheap and easy to do. It takes no special equipment and you can do it practically anywhere. I love to walk and run and have been practicing this form of conditioning for over 60 years. I try to walk or run five miles a day — more when I have time.

I rediscovered my competitive edge when I attended the International Fair Convention at Balley's Resort on the Las Vegas strip. The Fair Association was holding a special event for members. It was a one-mile run around the parking lot, to Harmon Street and back along the strip to Balley's (which used to be the M.G.M., but had been sold). I was in fair shape because I'd been running each night at my security job out on the Boulder Highway. I managed to win my age category and have kept at it, realizing the long-term health benefits.

Along with keeping my "motor" in good shape with exercise, I've also paid attention to the fuel. Food is so important to good health. I wholeheartedly believe that an apple a day keeps the doctor away. I strive to consume fruits, vegetables, cereal made from whole wheat and oats, plus milk and plenty of water. Variety and a balanced diet are the key, along with calcium and vitamins like C and E.

I grew up eating meat, potatoes and eggs, the fare most typical farm meals are built around. After I turned 50 I got away from meat and now get most of my protein from peanut butter. I also love beans, and the nutrition experts are backing me up on what I've learned works for me.

Luckily for me, I never got into drinking. While I don't have a problem with people who like a drink, it's never seemed necessary to me. I'm not quite so tolerant about smoking. Talk about a dirty, stupid, costly habit. I honestly don't know how smoking ever got so popular!

Sermon's over, folks. As you will soon discover, I'm no saint and I definitely don't have all the answers! Just ask my three ex-wives...

The prestigious International Association of Fairs and Expositions was one of the official organizations linking more than 3,000 fairs in the United States and Canada. Jack was a member for many years.

Jack performed at more fairs in Iowa than in any other state. Some of the good ones, such as the Clay County Fair in Spencer, and the Woodbury County Fair at Moville, were a few of Jack's favorites.

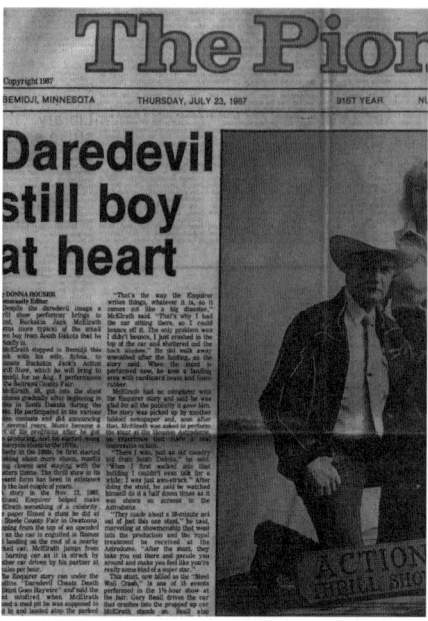

Top left: The Bemidji, MN, newspaper, carried a tremendous story on Jack and Sylvia. Jack was sporting a dandy mustache at the time!

Top right: Jack enjoyed the many fairs in Michigan. Jack had a $7,000 contract – which attracted attention from the IRS – at the Jackson County Fair. This fairgrounds was one of the most beautiful Jack saw during his cross-country travels.

Lower right: Jack was also a member of the Wisconsin Association of Fairs. These fairs were always a lot of fun in the summer.

Top left: A poster from Jack's Las Vegas Downs show in 1972.

Upper right: Clair Dunkelberger kept this ticket stub as a souvenir of his trip to Madison Square Garden in 1946. At that time, the rodeo lasted 30 days!

Lower left: A clipping from the Flint, MI, newspaper recaps Jack's performance at the Auto City Speedway.

Lower right: This Flying Buckskin Rodeo program book was prepared for the 1970 rodeo at the 1970 Sioux Falls Arena.

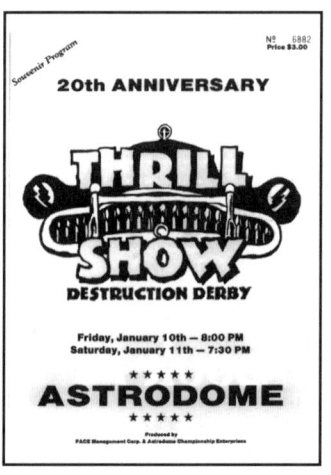
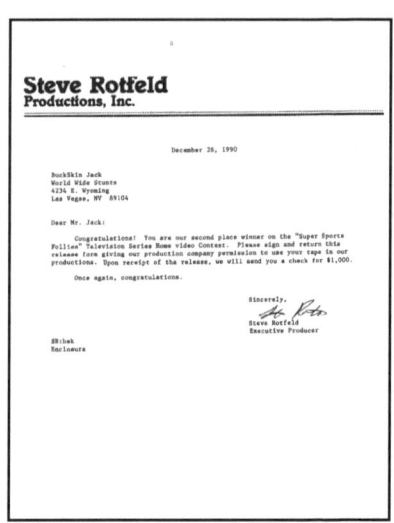
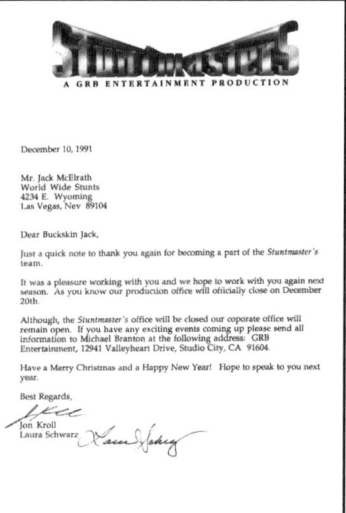

Top left: This poster announcing the Houston Thrill Show in 1986 reminds Jack of one of the highlights of career. More than 50,000 people crowded into the Houston Astrodome to see Jack and other national stunt people perform.

Top right: One of Jack's best deals ever! Jack sent a video of his stunts, the video was included in the *Super Sports Follies* and Jack received $1,000.

Left: Everything clicked when Jack worked with the *Stuntmasters*. The show was filmed at Husett's Speedway in 1991, and Jack appreciated his working relationship with the crew. The show is still beamed around the world and you can catch it occasionally.

Bottom: This postcard publicized the Spencer County Fair in 1988. Jack's stuntshow was a big hit at the Clay County Fair, one of the best county fairs in the country.

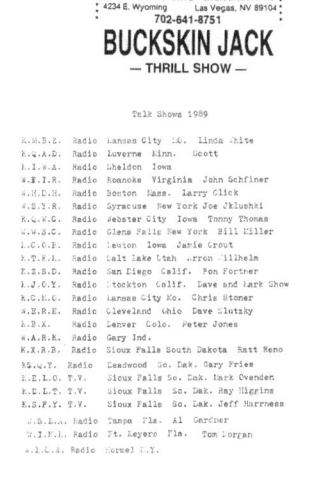
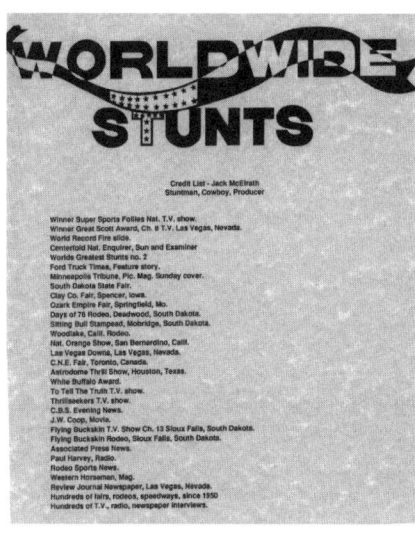

Top left and right: Jack used credit sheets like these to promote his show.

Lower left and right: The Argus Leader has followed Jack's exploits, from 1951 through 1997.

'I'm always thinking about what kind of stunt I can do next. I've been wanting to make a jump in one of those Pontiac Fieros. The engine's behind the front seat, so I think the nose would stay up higher longer.'
— Buckskin Jack McElrath, stuntman

Lew Sherman/ Argus Leader
Jack McElrath stands in his living room with his bull rope, used bull riding.

Stunt master Buckskin Jack is no stranger to risk taking

He's leaped off tops of cars, crashed through flaming walls and, at 63, he insists he's not quite finished yet

January on the Dakota landscape. The snowbirds have flown to Tempe and Palm Springs. And Jack McElrath is dreaming again.

But the 63-year-old Sioux Falls man's mind is a long ways from the desert southwest as he takes a shovel to the ice and snow caked on his driveway.

No, old Buckskin Jack — as he calls himself — is back in his stuntman mode again, imagining himself inside a Pontiac Fiero, hurling up a ramp at 60 miles an hour and soaring through the air as bombs explode around him.

"I'm always thinking about what kind of stunt I can do next," he said as he took a break and set aside the shovel.

STEVE YOUNG

Argus Leader columnist Steve Young writes about interesting people and events shaping our community. Ideas are welcome. Phone 331-2306 or write: Box 5034, Sioux Falls, SD 57117

"I've been wanting to make a jump in one of those Pontiac Fieros. The engine's behind the front seat, so I think the nose would stay up higher longer."

Sounds kind of crazy for a guy whose days are filled with working security at Menard's and jogging the bike trails on the dike behind the Great Plains Zoo.

But then Buckskin Jack is no stranger to the wild side. Who else do you know that has:

■ Wrestled steers after dropping out of low-flying airplanes.
■ Leapt off the top of an upright car as another vehicle barreled into it.
■ Slid 200 feet through burning hay while riding a scoop shovel.

"I've been called crazy since I was 10 years old," McElrath said as he dipped a tea bag into a cup of hot water. "But I tell you what, I just love it."

Now, he's hoping others will love it, too. McElrath is writing a book about his career as

Argus Leader columnist Steve Young captured Jack in this story and photo feature in early 1997. Steve's interest in Jack sparked an interest around the city in Jack's upcoming book, *The Cowboy Stuntman*.

Ford Truck Times Latches onto Flying Buckskin Story in the Spring 1967 Issue

SPINNING WHEELS AND FLYING HOOVES

A professional cowboy on the rodeo circuit does a lot of riding. Not all of it is on the backs of convulsed broncos or steers with the whammies. Jack and Karen McElrath spend a good deal of time riding in their Ford pickup. And for them its Twin-I-Beam ride is always a pleasant interlude.

—by HENRY & VERA BRADSHAW

Shooting arrows into a straw target while riding a pair of quarterhorses Roman style is hardly the way most people would spend a pleasant summer's evening. Fewer still would ever consider making a living this way. They'd probably settle for a trip to the moon first.

For Jack McElrath, however, this is bread and butter... part of a daily routine when he's on the rodeo circuit. And when his arrows are exhausted—to get back to the act—Jack maneuvers his buckskins over a two-foot hurdle... still riding Roman style. To top that, he literally ascends an 18-foot plank astride one of his ponies to a small platform atop his Ford pickup... and does a shoulder stand.

For someone like Jack, the thought of white-collar, bluecollar or collarless work of any sort away from horses and rodeos is as remote, unimaginable and upsetting as nine-to-five people are likely to find his work. His wife, Karen, feels the same way. And she proves it by the way she has learned to ride since she married Jack three years ago. Until then, a rodeo was strictly a spectator sport as far as she was concerned. Not any more. Now she's in the thick of every rodeo they attend, assisting Jack with his "Flying Buckskins" act... and bringing home her share of the prize money from the ladies' events.

Left: Jack adjusts a stirrup for his wife, Karen... who has taken to rodeo life like a duck to water. She never rode a horse before she married Jack three years ago. Top, left: The trailer is home for the McElraths when they're on the road. Here they enjoy hot coffee after tough day performing at a rodeo. Top, right: Jack stands beside his wonderhorse, Bob, who is quite a pet. Horses get plenty of tender, loving care from Jack and Karen. Center: This Ford F-250 pickup hauls all of Jack McElrath's worldly possessions. His horses, known as the Flying Buckskins, travel in the back of the truck. He and Karen call the trailer "home," and so does Heidi, their German shepherd dog.

Every Ford truck owner in the United States received this *Ford Truck Times* featuring Jack and Karen and the Flying Buckskins. This article in the Spring 1967 issue was photographed in Sioux Falls, SD.

Jack, himself, is recognized as a top radio announcer by the Association of Rodeo Cowboys of America. And he works at it regularly in season. But first and foremost, he's an all-around rodeo performer who often leaves his microphone to board a hard-bucking bronco.

When they're following the summer rodeo circuit, the McElraths carry all their worldly possessions along with them. Matter of fact, the husky F-250 Ford pickup featured in their act totes the two buckskin horses, Bob and Buck, in the roomy rear compartment. It also pulls the 25-foot blue and silver trailer the McElraths call home. Many of their friends travel the same way. So life at the trailer camps on the grounds of any rodeo is always like "old home week" for them.

In the off-season, the McElraths keep themselves and their horses trim by practicing their regular acts and creating new ones. They do this on a few acres of land they own just outside Sioux Falls, South Dakota. But they move around quite a bit in the winter, too. Matter of fact, the McElraths will tell you that home really doesn't feel like home to them anymore unless they can hitch their Ford pickup to it and take it wherever they go . . . whenever they feel like going. ∎

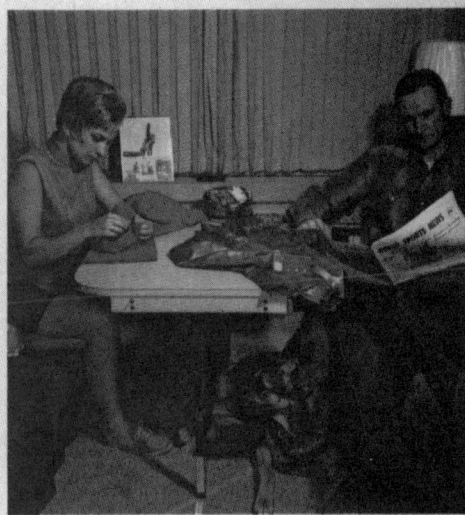

Bottom left: Climax of Jack's rodeo act comes when he climbs 18-foot ramp astride Bob. While horse stands quietly on 5x10-ft. perch, Jack does a handstand on the horse's back. On the road, ramp rides under the trailer. Above: "There's no place like home"...is what the McElraths say as they relax during the evening in their trailer home.

Diary entry dated September 4, 1968, Sioux Falls, SD

One day I stopped at KSOO TV and talked to Mel Heath, the program director. I wanted to do a show on rodeo and farm events, both local and national. Mel liked the concept and The Flying Buckskin Show went on the air that fall. It was a 30-minute show that began at noon on Saturdays and ran from 1968 to 1971. I was the host — Buckskin Jack McElrath — and my wife Karen was also involved. Karen and I married in 1963 and she was good with animals and training.

The show was fun and I worked on it the whole time, filming at every location I visited each year. I carried a handheld camera that used 16 millimeter film with me at all times. I shot some footage and Glenn Wentzel also did a fair amount. This was well before the advent of video cameras. We even covered the National Finals Rodeo in Oklahoma City in 1968 and 1969.

I sold advertisements and had plenty of sponsors. Haegle's Western Store, the Western Mall and Ben-Hur Ford were loyal sponsors.

Chapter 8
Look Out, Kirk Douglas!

Riding horses Roman style is a real trick, as you might have guessed from countless Hollywood movies where actors stand atop running horses, but then the Flying Buckskins were special. I started in 1963 with Bob and Buck, buckskin-colored quarter horses. I wanted a special act to work rodeos and knew that standing up on two running horses would be perfect.

First I hooked a 16-inch strap from one cinch to another, holding the horses together. Then I stood up on soft saddle pads placed on Bob's and Buck's backs. We first walked, then trotted for long rides. Soon the two horses would stay side by side without being tied together. Take it from me: running wide open around an arena was fun and great way to stay in shape!

Buck, who was a bit taller, was on the right side and Bob was on the left. Because of Buck's height, I liked to have him on the outside of the circle. Pretty soon we got good enough to begin doing other stunts. One we did real well was the Mix-up. Bob would turn toward Buck and spin all the way around. My long legs helped make this work. We used this trick through the 1960s and '70s, from Midwest rodeos to as far away as San Bernardino, California.

1974 was an especially good year. The ensemble that year consisted of Kyle Evans and his band providing music and Kyle doing some motorcycle stunts, La Costa Tucker singing — her hit record *Get on the Love Train* was hot and fans were wild for her — me doing the horse and highland bull act and Dee Dee Ortman, Liz Olsen and Miss South

Dakota Gina Campbell helping out with the acts. We performed about 30 times at county fairs throughout the Midwest.

We even appeared in the movie, *J.W. Coop*, in 1970. If you like Cliff Robertson, don't expect to see any disco dancing and can stand to see me come in second in a horse race, you might want to rent the video some time...

Actually, I was part of the Professional Rodeo Cowboys Association and I had pulled into a California ranch during the summer of 1970. A film crew was working, so I tracked down what was going on. Cliff Robertson was starring and producing and it didn't take me long to get acquainted with Cliff. He decided to put the Flying Buckskins in the horse race. Cliff would ride one and I'd ride the other. I was all set to be a movie star. The story was for 12 of us to vault on our horses, race out of the arena, swim a lake, race over a hill and back again into the arena. We filmed this over and over until we got it right.

Naturally, Cliff "J.W. Coop" was first and I was second. At least the announcer mentioned my name no less than three times. I can still hear John Jackson announcing now, "Buckskin Jack McElrath is in second place!" It was a nice credit to have playing all over the world.

I'm still surprised occasionally when I catch a clip from a movie or a TV show that features one of my stunts. One cold night in December 1996 I was watching television when I stumbled across a program called *The World's Greatest Stunts*. I was the lead stunt, jumping off the auto in the Steel Wall Crash. I got a kick out of seeing that stunt, and the timing was ironic. I had been working hard on writing this book that fall and winter, dredging up memories and experiences and trying to make sense of a life given over to thrills, stunts and danger.

I realized again that there is a part of us that is drawn to danger's allure. We like to watch Evil Knievel or Harry

Houdini, usually from the safety of our Lay-Z-Boys or the grandstand. And then there are those of us who feel compelled to provide the danger, conjure up the magic that entrances you. It really isn't something that you get over or recover from, like an illness, because it's as much a part of you as the color of your eyes or the cowlicks on the back of your head. There's no use fighting it by getting a nice, safe job installing automatic dishwashers. You go with it, give your nature its head, and hold on as your life gallops away with you.

Diary entry dated September 22, 1954, Sioux Falls, SD

    Kitty Halde and I had horses during our school days and were very involved in the Junior Saddle Club. Kitty and I ran into each other again while I was in the Air Force. It felt so good to hold onto normal things when you were in such extraordinary situations. When I came home on leave in 1954 we said "I do" at a church in Luverne, MN. Don Merrill was the best man.

Chapter 9
It Wasn't All Wine and Roses

Relationships. I was really good at starting them, and I always managed to finish them, but I just couldn't get the hang of sustaining them. This was nobody's fault but my own, for all three of my wives were great ladies. Maybe my lifestyle and travel — to construction jobs and rodeos and motorsports — wore away at the glue that held us together. Or it might have been inattention, scarcity of money, lack of a stable place to hang our hats. You probably have to stay a bit closer to home than I ever did. Maybe I'm too much of a cowboy, always riding off into the sunset with my horse!

Kitty Halde and I were Junior Horseman Club buddies back in high school. I thought Kitty was a bit out of my league when she went to Stephens Girls College in Columbia, MO, but I really admired her horsemanship. She showed English-style at horse shows in the Midwest. I was back on leave from the Air Force in the fall of 1954 and we started dating. She was engaged and about to marry a fellow who worked for her dad. She had her doubts and decided to call off the wedding.

One night we got carried away and I told Kitty that if I had anything to offer I'd ask her to go back to California with me. She said, "Why don't you ask?!" Our marriage took place September 22, 1954, at the Methodist Church in Luverne, MN.

It turned out that I got more than I asked for with Kitty. I returned to California right after the wedding and Kitty came out a month later. I think she had to tell her Dad she had gotten married. I found an apartment in Valejo and enjoyed the first few weeks of married life. Kitty told me as soon as she arrived that she was pregnant. I wasn't certain who the father was, but I said it was all right.

Mark McElrath was born at the base hospital on May 22, 1955. Kitty had to go back to the hospital for a week, though, because of an infection. So there I was, taking care of Mark. Bottles, diapers and the whole routine. I was so nervous with my tiny son I broke out in a rash. It was quite a week!

I was happy to return home to South Dakota when I was discharged from the Air Force in 1956. My father-in-law, Fred Halde, was a lathing and plastering contractor with work all over the Midwest. Home was Sioux Falls, but I worked in South Dakota, North Dakota, Minnesota, Iowa and Nebraska. It turned out that the rodeo and construction trades were complementary businesses and the lathing trade worked out well for the next 20 years.

Unfortunately, the marriage didn't work out quite so well. The union lasted from 1954 till 1961 and was a lot of fun. I mean that sincerely. Thinking back to the seven years with Kitty, I realize they were very good.

We had a new horse trailer and a palomino horse and spent summers on the rodeo trail. I was riding and bulldogging while Kitty was barrel racing and working as a timer. We even bought an 80-acre place south of Sioux Falls for $3,000. It was a mess but for that kind of money you couldn't go wrong. We moved our trailer and started to fix up the place. What a project! The barn had two to three feet of hard manure, there was bad fencing and junk all over the place. Even the shed was falling down. Kitty's dad helped me put a new roof on the barn and I painted it. We put up new fences and Dad sent about 200 sheep to clean up the weeds. When the time came to sell the property, we doubled our investment.

I guess our marital problems came down to being too

busy and out of town too much. I simply didn't appreciate Kitty at the time and just let her get away. She fell in love and finally told me she wanted a divorce. I didn't want one and told her so, but there was no hope of changing her mind. I packed up and moved out.

A divorce at its very best is a bad situation. You've failed; there's no way around that fact. After the separation I cried, felt sorry for myself and just ran around in circles for a while. A few weeks went by and I made up my mind that it would be fun to be single again and do as I pleased. I wanted to rodeo and now I could really go at it. In fact, the more I thought about it, the better I liked the idea.

I recovered by driving my 1956 truck out to Las Vegas to stay with my sister Jan. We went to shows and dinners and enjoyed Las Vegas to the hilt. My first show experience was the Lido at the Stardust. You needed to call ahead for reservations, get there around 6 p.m. and stand in long time before being seated.

I was enjoying my steak when the show started right on time. I almost dropped my fork when I saw the nude girls walking down the stairs in the opening production number. But I quickly recovered, enjoying a fantastic show with fireworks and waterworks.

I spent the winter months there in Vegas, working as a lather on the airport terminal addition and bulldogging on weekends. That summer I went back to South Dakota, traded my truck for a new 1962 Ford pickup and camper. It was a good summer for rodeoing, leading up to another fateful, romantic summer.

I met Karen Seefong in Beaver Falls, PA, in 1963. She was a fan at a rodeo there and I was a contestant. Karen was a beautiful 19-year-old from Canton, OH. She had a deep summer tan and I sure noticed her sitting on the top of the fence, looking at the stock. We dated and enjoyed the lake and surrounding area. I had to go to Manawa, WI, for a rodeo the next weekend. Karen drove her old Mercury over there to see me. Then it was on to Sioux Falls ... and on and on till 1975! Actually, within two weeks we were Mr. and Mrs. When my Mom asked what my intentions were, I told her I thought we might get married. I almost decided against it, but when I tried to tell Karen she cried and was all broken up. I melted and said OK. That was a mistake. I should have sent her home. Two weeks isn't really not long enough to get acquainted, but I just wasn't tough enough to love them and leave them.

This impulsive behavior just goes to show what stupid decisions we sometimes make. I had 10 years to make the best of it, but there's no way to make a good deal out of a bad deal. Actually, Karen had many redeeming qualities. She loved animals and was a very good trainer. She was lovely to look at but, to borrow a phrase from my teenage co-workers at my current security job, often an airhead. Karen also wanted a house and security, two things that I wasn't capable of providing on a long-term basis.

For two years Karen and I lived on a five-acre place south of Sioux Falls. We lived in a travel trailer and I built a 16-foot-by-24-foot cabin onto it. The cabin had open beams and a fireplace. Actually I had only wanted to put a 4-foot-by-6-foot entry on the trailer, but Karen put the push on me and we ended up putting $1,000 worth of material in the cabin and still didn't have an entry.

Once while I was gone, a doctor who lived two blocks from us came over and asked Karen for a livestock water tank he said belonged to him. Karen said he was a little drunk and gave her a bad time. She said he tore his pants climbing the through the fence, but he said Karen turned our dog Heidi on him and the dog tore his pants. In any event, he called the sheriff and we went to court over the incident. I finally got it settled by buying him a new pair of pants. I never knew for sure who to believe. Karen was angry with me because I doubted her. Thinking back, she was probably right.

    By the fall of 1975 things had pretty much fallen apart. I called her to ask if we were married or not. I had signed divorce papers during the summer after carrying them around for several months and had finally returned them to Karen. I never thought she'd go through with it, but she did.

    I was single from 1975 to 1981 and really enjoyed the single life. I traveled to shows all over Canada and the Midwest. Then in 1979 I took a security job at the Western Hotel and Casino in Las Vegas. Sylvia Garbati started working there at about the same time as a cocktail waitress in the casino. I escorted her to her Jeep at midnight when her shift was over, but she never smiled and didn't have much to say.

    I asked her one night if things were really that bad and she said yes. Her husband was just one big fight and her three teenage children were having trouble with him. He was her second husband and not their father. So I listened to these troubles for about a year.

    I really liked Sylvia; she was such a nice person. I never saw her get mad or raise her voice to anyone. She was a great worker, too, always early and treated the casino players like family. Everyone loved Sylvia, including me.

    Then Sylvia divorced and times were much better around her house. We dated a lot and I felt we were the perfect couple. In 1981 a shaky old justice of the peace in Las Vegas pronounced us man and wife. I had 10 great years with Sylvia and her kids. We enjoyed the shows, country music and life was great.

    However, being out on the road doing summer shows was not so great. Sylvia could only get two weeks of vacation and I was out for three to four months. The road life took its toll on the marriage, and when Sylvia boarded the plane at Grand Rapids, MI, after bookings in the Ozarks, Iowa and

Michigan in the summer of 1990, I had the feeling it would never be the same again. It wasn't. We drifted apart and divorced in 1991. I can only say good things about Sylvia, who was the love of my life.

    Now I'm back to the single life and it's probably best for me. I enjoy a good relationship, but see no reason to be married if you aren't happy. There's a lot to be said for each lifestyle. Life is too short to be unhappy with what you do — whether it's your personal or professional life.

Gunman kills guard amid heist

☐ Lounge patrons say the 53-year-old Navy veteran, Eugene Bradford, tried in vain to stop the robbery.

By Alonza Robertson
Review-Journal

A security guard killed early Monday while trying to intervene in a robbery at a Las Vegas lounge was being praised as a hero who always pitched in when needed.

"We want everyone to know this guy was a hero in this whole incident," said Connie Brennan, a spokeswoman for Sportsman's Bait & Lounge, 5660 Boulder Highway.

Upset co-workers described Eugene Bradford, 53, a U.S. Navy veteran, as a congenial gentleman, always willing to help. Since May 1993, he was a full-time employee of the lounge.

"A lot of people here were pretty close to him and they're taking this pretty tough," said Patrick Fiedeke, a controller with Sportsman's. "There was no way not to like him, he really was an exceptional man."

Bradford lived on the property with his fiancee. A spring wedding, his first marriage, was planned for this year, Fiedeke said.

Bradford was pronounced dead on arrival at University Medical Center after he was found critically wounded about 2:45 a.m. by Las Vegas police near the entrance of the lounge.

Witnesses told police a man entered the 24-hour lounge from a rear door and approached the main bar area, firing shots and ordering everyone to the floor. The man jumped the bar counter

Please see GUARD/3B

Diary entry dated January 6, 1991, Las Vegas, NV

The 20 years of security work in Las Vegas have been loaded with exciting events. I could have lived without some of them... After years downtown and out on the strip, I spent five years at the Sportsman's Resort out on the Boulder Highway.

The first night on duty a knife fight broke out between two men and security was called to break it up. The other security man and I got it under control. After we shipped one of the fighters off to the hospital with a knife wound, my partner turned to me and said "You probably don't think much of this job!" But I kept showing up each night at 9 and worked until 5. It wasn't long before he was gone and I was on duty alone each night, looking out for a bar, gas station, store and 200-unit motel and apartment complex covering five acres.

Chapter 10
Dead Men Don't Make Much Money

"Bang!" A shot flew past my head from a .38 handgun just 30 feet away. I could smell the gun powder in the early morning air of Las Vegas. The gunman was sitting in his white Camaro, backed into a parking space in front of the Sportsman's Bar.

I had walked around the corner and I guess my security uniform must have spooked him. He fired, then put the pedal to the metal and took off down the Boulder Highway.

Unusual event? Not really. I had faced events like this many times in my 20 years of security work. But this isn't exactly the kind of danger I expected to face as I was growing up, planning to be an Iowa farmer. Twenty-three years in Las Vegas had changed my perspective though, especially after my security partner was gunned down at the very same bar in January 1994.

Eugene Bradford's death was one of those things I never expected to happen. There were plenty of bar fights and domestic quarrels. In fact, one night a shotgun blast narrowly missed a lady's head and blew apart a wall. There were plenty of fights between redneck construction workers. It's amazing that I didn't get hurt many times, and I believe that my background as a bronc rider and stuntman helped me deal with the physical and mental work-outs involved with security jobs.

People just love to gamble, which is the main reason I had a security job to begin with, but what they do at casinos goes far beyond wagering. People in general live very boring lives. When they break up their routine by setting foot in the exciting world of a casino, their style undergoes a total transformation. The casinos capitalize on this with plenty of free drinks and showmanship. Even security men who move around in uniform, packing a .38 special and bringing thousands of dollars in chips to a table, add to the excitement. There's the thrill of betting on the turn of a card, the roll of the dice, or the spin of the wheel.

The dashing dealers, both male and female, and the sexy cocktail waitresses add to atmosphere. Most people don't care if they win or lose. They just want to play the game for a while and be part of this world.

It isn't any wonder, then, why casinos and hotels pull in so much money. They are providing the thrills people are seeking. Working in a casino is a show unto itself. Most drunks are very entertaining, but once in a while someone gets hostile and threatening. My job was to watch the crowds and spot trouble before it happens. It's amazing how good you get at picking out troublemakers.

Robberies, assaults and break-ins happen every day. I didn't have to draw my weapon very often, but I had my moments. There was a regular customer who came in two or three nights a week. One night he got to drinking too much, got loud and belligerent, disturbing other customers. Finally the pit boss told me to 86 the man (when you tell an individual that he's 86ed, it means he must leave and isn't allowed to come back) and make sure he didn't come back. I proceeded to tell him as nicely as possible. He went out, only to come right back in and start yelling at the pit boss. Once again I got him outside, but he hung around the front door, making derogatory comments about the casino to anyone who would listen. I tried to get him to leave, but the pit boss finally asked me to call the police. They arrived and threatened to take him to jail unless he left. He left.

A week later the same guy came back with his brother

and some friends. I reminded him of the 86 order. He said it had been lifted and everything was OK. I had no information on this, but gave him the benefit of the doubt. When I checked later I discovered that the order was still in effect. He came again the following night. I told him he had conned me and he must leave for good. He went angrily, calling me several colorful names in the process.

Again the next night, the same guy came with his brother and eight or nine friends. They gathered around the crap table just to see how much noise and mayhem them could create. They left and I hoped that would be the end of it. But they showed up again around 3 a.m., ordering more drinks and giving us a bad time. They went to the 21 table, tipping over chairs and being obnoxious. The fellow who started the ordeal by being 86ed was outside the front door, cheering them on. The boss hit the table twice with his fist and told them to back off. I was right there, ready to do what I could and hoping whatever I did was right.

The real problem with this situation was that these guys were employees of a hotel and casino down the street, owned by the same group as the one where I was working. I called over there, asking for one of their security guys to show up. He did and once again they left and I heaved a sigh of relief. The next morning my pickup was covered with orange sticky stuff. I wondered if there was any connection.

One Saturday night the casino was quite full, and I had just come on duty. I was watching the exits and parking areas when a dealer came out and said they had a problem in the pit.

When I moved into the pit, the boss told me a fellow had pulled a knife out of his sock and threatened the boss. Then he had left, stating that he would be back with a gun to kill him and then burn the place down.

About 1,000 people had hit the floor when the guy pulled the knife, thinking he had a gun. We never saw the guy again; however, I spent the night keeping a close watch on the pit and the exits. I went into the security business knowing there would be trouble, yet hoping to avoid any tragedies.

But security work was steady every September through May, the "off-season" for Buckskin Jack McElrath and his steady diet of rodeos, stunt shows, motorsports, and country music shows from June through September. This was *showtime* — from the Houston Astrodome to Toronto, Canada, from coast to coast and border to border and a thousand places in between — and what I loved to do best.

What drove me to lead this fractured life? Perhaps it was the travel. Maybe the adventure, attention, showing off or just an ego trip. It could be fame and fortune. Who knows? It could be all of it. But I've had 63 years to mull over my motivations and I think it really comes down to having fun. After all, my idea of a good time is riding a bull or horse. I like to bulldog a steer, jump a stunt auto or slide 200 feet through an inferno. In fact, I may be an old fool, but I've decided to participate in the bull riding exhibition in June at the Sioux Falls fairgrounds. My old buddy Bob Barnes is providing stock for the firefighters rodeo there. Somehow it only seems fitting that the world's oldest bull rider is Buckskin Jack McElrath.

I like to talk about stunts on the radio or appear in a movie or show up on TV. The unusual has a special allure for me because I like to *live* life, not just be a spectator.

For all these reasons, I was gladly living the dual life of stuntman/security guard. I know that dead security guards don't make much money — and frankly, neither do stuntmen — but this was the life I loved.

Parade photo by Ken Jones of the Las Vegas Sun; all other photos from Jack's private collection

Top, left: Jack, Kitty and Mark McElrath enjoy a few moments at home in 1955.

Top, right: Karen and Jack attend the Spooner, WI, rodeo in 1964, where Jack was the announcer.

Center left: Karen rides Bob while Jack discusses his latest failed attempt at skydogging in the desert near Las Vegas.

Lower left: Karen and Jack goof around at Jack's folks' home in 1964.

Lower right: Karen and Jack ride Shag and Scotty in the Helldorado Parade at Las Vegas, NV, in 1973. They were presented with a beautiful trophy for this parade entry.

Top left: Country music fans Jack and Sylvia pose for a photo session at Sam's Town in Las Vegas.

Top right: Gary Beall, Sylvia and Jack prepare for their stunt show at Rock Rapids, IA, in 1988.

Left center: Sylvia and her children Shawn and Crystal, who worked Jack's shows, clown around.

Right center: Sylvia with the stunt car in Las Vegas in 1990.

Lower right: The whole crew at a show close to Beaver, UT, in 1983.

Lower left: Sylvia clothes herself in leather to ride her Harley Davidson in Las Vegas in 1990.

All photos from Jack's private collection

Top left: Tanya Tucker gave Jack one of her first publicity photos from Bruno of Hollywood in 1973.

Top right: La Costa Tucker's song, "Get on My Love Train," wowed Jack's fans during their 40 performances in the summer of 1974.

Lower left: La Costa is now president of Tanya's fan club, Brentwood, TN, and a great singer in her own right.

Lower right: Singer Judy Lynn worked with Jack in the '70s. She as an outstanding showperson, singing and rodeoing. Her husband John Kelly booked Jack's shows.

Photos from La Costa's and Judy's private collections

Upper left: Jack enjoyed working security for singer Mac Davis's performances at the MGM Grand in 1983.

Center: The greatest stuntman of all time, Evil Knievel, parked his rig in Las Vegas in 1984.

Right: Jack and Dottie West became friends during her performances at the MGM Grand in 1983-84. Dottie was killed in an automobile accident while on her way to the Grand Ole Opry in 1991.

Evil Knievel photo from Jack's private collection; Mac Davis from Rogers & Cowan, Inc.; Dottie West photo from Ken Kragen of Kragen Companies

Top left: Catherine Bach is a South Dakota girl, hailing from Faith. Her family was involved in rodeo, so she fit right into her western clothes. She and Jack had plenty to talk about when Catherine was a guest at the MGM Grand. Jack zeroed right in on her, asking if her real name was Bachman. Jack used to rodeo with her uncle, Eddie Bachman.

Top right: Academy-Award winning movie star Cliff Robertson braved the South Dakota cold to appear with Jack at the premier of his movie, *JW Coop*. Jack played a role in the movie, coming in second to Cliff during a horse race. Each rode one of the Flying Buckskins, while announcer Johnny Jackson proclaimed their progress. Fans can still see the movie on TV.

Right: A very special lady, Barbara Mandrell, treated Jack like family while she was security for her at the MGM Grand.

Barbara Mandrell's photo by Dick Blake Agency; Catherine Bach photo from National Enquirer; Cliff Robertson photo from Argus Leader

Upper left: LaWanda Linsey and Jack worked a number of shows together. LaWanda is from Bakersfield, CA.

Upper right: Miss South Dakota 1976 Gina Campbell hailed from Canton, SD. She sang in many of Jack's shows in the mid-70s.

Center left: Liz Olson poses on the Flying Buckskins in the practice arena in Las Vegas. Liz was so skilled that she could ride while holding a bottle of Coca-Cola.

Lower left: Kyle Evans and his band are from Wessington Springs, SD. They worked a lot of rodeos, and were special to Jack. Great musicians with lots of intelligence, unlike many bands, they stayed close to home.

Lower right: Bonnie Nelson, a beautiful lady and great talent, worked some of Jack's shows. She's from Nashville, TN.

All photos from Jack's private collection, except Liz Olson's photo, taken by Ken Jones of the Las Vegas Sun

Top left: Gale and Shane Anderson posed for this shot at Cadillac, MI. Shane is now one of the nation's best bullfighters and rodeo clowns.

Top center: Artist Ray Kelly of Tea, SD, appeared as Flyspeck Kelly at the Custer, SD, theater.

Top right: Karla Aman Laackman performed stunts on Jack's show for about three years.

Lower left: Lola Jean Dillon and Dee Dee Ortman worked Jack's show for several years. Lola Jean was a singer and songwriter, who penned the Loretta Lynn hit "When the Tingle Turns to a Chill."

Lower right: Doug "9 Toes" Marble of Mankato, MN, thrilled the fans at Jack's shows with his Harley Davidson firewall crashes.

All photos from Jack's private collection

All photos from Jack's private collection

Clockwise, from top left: Weatherman Ken Hirsch loves to announce at air shows. Having announced the national show at Osh Kosh, WI, Ken also heads up the Sioux Falls shows. Ken has even branched out into the travel business.

Denny Oviatt announced many of Jack's shows, going way back into the '60s. Denny worked at KSOO in Sioux Falls, SD, for many years, and encouraged Jack to the skydogging stunt while on the air. Local fans identify with Denny's announcing talents at Husett's Speedway.

Ed Pillar was promoter, salesman, Ford dealer, and politician extraordinaire. He even took one of his trick mules to the Democratic convention one year.

Merle Ostgaard, junior saddle club advisor in the late '40s and early '40s, is still going strong.

Bob Barnes has been in the rodeo business 50 years, not only producing rodeos but also supplying top stock at the National Finals Rodeo. Bob has helped Jack over the years, giving him breaks as an announcer, performing specialty acts and featuring the Flying Buckskins at many shows. In this 1991 photo, Bob has stopped by Jack's booth at the MGM Grand in Las Vegas just to say howdy.

Former Gov. Frank Farrar, from Britton, SD, was a big booster for Jack and the Flying Buckskin Rodeo.

The Suttons are pioneer ranchers, rodeo producers and stock contractors from Onida, SD. This family is a fixture in South Dakota rodeo circles, respected by citizens across the state.

Jack worked for the family on the ranch in the winter of 1964-65 and went on to ride and announce at many of their rodeos. The Suttons furnished stock for the Flying Buckskin Rodeo in Sioux Falls and in 1997 furnished the stock for the Intercollegiate Rodeo Finals in Rapid City, SD. Each year top-Sutton stock appears in the National Finals Rodeo.

Steve Sutton has been pickup man many times at the finals in Las Vegas. They furnish stock for many of the established rodeos in the Midwest.

All photos from rodeo programs

Top: Don Merrill presented Tanya Tucker with a Gelbvieh calf in 1973. Tanya was interested in the cattle business and Gelbvieh cattle were just becoming popular in the U.S. at that time.

Right: Bette Ketchem Riddlestene was one of Jack's riding friends and an advisor to the riding club in Sioux Falls. Bette's horse Topper and dog Pal were constant companions in the 1940s. She now lives in Mauston, WI, where Bette and her husband are dairy farmers.

Top right: Jack's rodeo buddy since 1945, Don Merrill rides a bareback bronc at Ben Brune's arena in 1950. On the left in the photo is one of Jack's great junior saddle club advisors, Ray Dunkelberger. Ray helped Jack many times over the years as Jack continued in the rodeo business.

Center: Ben Brune used his business card as a receipt in 1943, when Clair Dunkelberger bought a horse. Ben was responsible for getting rodeos established in Sioux Falls in the 1940s. He made it possible for city kids to experience cowboy life. Dennis Reiners, 1970 world champion saddle bronc rider, got his start at Brune's arena.

Lower right: Ben Brune was the focus of a newspaper story. He worked until the day he died, helping others and living a full life. Ben was laid to rest after a cowboy funeral in Salem, SD.

Lower left: Velda Brune and Donna Hansen bear the flags during the grand entry of a Brune rodeo.

Top photo from Argus Leader; all others from Clair Dunkelberger's collection

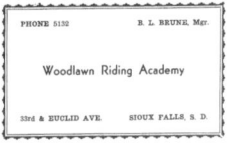

Top left: Hollywood stuntman Gary Beall visits Jack in Las Vegas to help promote their show at the International Fair Convention at the MGM Grand in 1988.

Top center: Jack and Barbara Carlson at Alden, MN, promoting the show at Owatonna, MN, in 1993. Jack has had the pickup in the background for nearly 30 years, proving that Ford trucks last longer.

Top right: Lucky Lott of Toronto was one of the all-time great auto stuntmen. He is shown here with a 1946 Ford stunt car.

Center: Jerry Olson of Fruitdale, SD, one of the all-time great rodeo clowns, bull-fighters, Roman riding, and buffalo acts, is now a South Dakota rancher. His son, Jerry Wayne, carries on the tradition.

Lower left: Jack's friend Jim Devlin from Pieoche, NV, worked stunts and construction together for many years. Jack was driving the jeep and clown John Guertin rode in the back.

Bottom: Las Vegas biker Pete Congar is a country music fan and booster for stunt shows.

All photos from Jack's private collection

> May 2nd 1997
>
> Dear Jack,
> I will be at your book signings. Do you like my picture that I drew? When is your birthday? Would you write every day to me? How old are you? Alot of question marks.
>
> A 8 YEAR OLD FAN!
>
> Love, Jordan

Upper left: Jack has watched Austin Merrill, grandson of Don and Alyce Merrill, grow from a toddler to a runner. Here, Austin tries on Jack's hat and boots.

Right: Isaac, Taryn and Jordan Gerdes, children of Nancy and Mark Gerdes, are fans of Jack's. One of Jordan's letters is shown above. The Gerdes family lives in Sioux Falls.

All photos from Jack's private collection

Clockwise from top left: Darlien "Dit" Goin enjoyed several rodeo adventures with Jack and Chuck Elshire in 1952. Dit and Jack still keep in touch.

Brian Edwards performs the fire tunnel jump at Beaver, UT, in 1983.

Glenn Wentzel of Sioux Falls, SD, is one of Jack's boosters and a friend since 1947. Glenn examines one of the props before a stunt show.

Jack, with a bandaged chin, Kenny Carlson and Don Merrill celebrate the conclusion of Jack's tremendous auto jump and crash at Rock Rapids, IA. Jack escaped with the loss of only one tooth.

Jack, Alyce and Don Merrill visit Fred Peterson's 60th birthday party in Flandreau, SD.

All photos from Jack's private collection

Diary entry dated July 4, 1948, Sioux Falls, SD

Bull riding started on a big white bull called Tarzan. The contest ride is for eight seconds and I was close the first time. After that it was on the road to Ben's summer rodeos in Minnesota and Wisconsin. I loved animals and wanted to stay around horses after leaving the Iowa farm. I wanted to be a cowboy!

At that time, they were small exhibition-type rodeos and not all of them were contests. You were paid $5 to ride a bareback horse or a bull. You got $7.50 for a saddle bronc, so I started riding saddle broncs and continued to enter contests until I was 55 years old.

Steer wrestling was the next event I tried and this worked out well over the years. I had many fast wins of 3.2-3.7 and under 5 seconds lots of times. Ben needed an announcer at his rodeos and I turned out to be the man behind the mike many times by sheer default. Ben's wife Velda helped me with announcing and became a dear friend of mine.

Chapter 11
One Minute I was Riding Steers and the Next Minute Rubbing Elbows with Stars

Working with animals and other cowboys in dusty arenas is one thing, working with glitzy stars in the smoke-filled glamour of Vegas is quite another. I didn't think much of it at the time, but it was a big leap from humble sweat, carefully timed danger and creaking leather to grease paint, silicone implants and Hollywood egos.

Working in Las Vegas put me in pretty close proximity with performers over the years, and you can always see their true natures emerge when they're not on stage. You can tell who's on drugs, who's got woes that overshadow their lives and who's a truly nice human being. Must be something in the dry desert air or the bright neon lights or the sharp distinction between a megawatt smile that doesn't quite the reach the eyes and the naturally friendly grin.

Since I wasn't really part of this world in the sense that I was not a celebrity, but shared the same drive to perform, it was fairly easy for me to detect a person's inner workings. And working security duty at places like M.G.M. gave me ample opportunity to meet and talk with the stars of the day.

There are stars. And then there are **STARS**. Barbara Mandrell, for instance, is a favorite. I worked security at her shows in 1983 and '84. She was just like a long-time friend, giving me coffee and sandwiches and making me feel welcome. We talked a lot about county fairs and the people we'd worked with. She was interested in what I was doing and treated me like a family member.

Tanya Tucker and her sister La Costa worked my show and I love them. Not only are they talented, but they're

REAL. I met Tanya back when she was 13. She, her brother Don, La Costa and their parents Beau and Juanita were living in a trailer in Henderson, NV, in 1972-73. I was in the area to promote my show at Las Vegas Downs. Joan Guertin introduced us and I invited Tanya out to ride my buckskins. Tanya loved horses and came on out for a ride. She even invited me to her birthday party. Her first big hit, *Delta Dawn*, came out about then but stardom didn't stop her from attending my show, riding and helping out. In 1974, La Costa sang at 40 performances of my show at Midwestern fairs. This is a fabulous family and we've kept in touch.

There were nice men, too. Mac Davis also entertained at the M.G.M., especially in 1982-83. He wore a leather jacket and Levis or Wranglers. He was just one of the guys off stage, and I liked him a lot. Dottie West opened his show wearing skin-tight britches, tall cowboy boots and a six gun and holster. Mac commented to me once that if she farted she would blow her boots off! Dottie was quite a talker. She talked in the room, on the way to the stage and out in the casino in the early afternoon. Dottie West was killed in an auto accident on her way to perform at the Grand Old Oprey in 1991.

Working in the M.G.M. gave me access to the stars, but they also had ways of shielding themselves if they didn't feel like having company.

Clint Eastwood walked into the casino one afternoon when I was on security duty. I said, "Hi, Bronco Billy." He stopped and looked down at me — he's 6'4" and I'm 6' — and said, "Did you like that movie?" I said, "Yes, it's one of my favorites. I've watched it six or seven times." Then Clint said, "Good. I liked it, too, and I put a lot into that one." Then he signed a photo for me, which I still have. What a guy!

Liberace was a flamboyant showman, and you could tell he loved what he was doing on stage. I probably watched him perform more than anybody else. I've never seen costumes like his before or since — long fur capes with rhinestones and jewels. He used special effects like the dancing waters backdrop that made his a spectacular show. I escorted Liberace from his dressing room for two shows each night, but there was something weird about being one-on-one with him! He didn't speak to me and I didn't talk to him.

I was really sad when Dean Martin died in 1996. Wow! They didn't get any better than Dean. He always shook my hand at the M.G.M. and asked how I was doing. He honestly cared about my answer! Dean had exercise equipment in his rooms at the hotel and worked out each day. He liked to talk about his horses or sports. I really don't think he drank much, even though that was part of his act, but he did smoke too many Kent cigarettes.

And then there's Cliff Robertson, a movie star and real friend. What fun it was to work with him in his movie, *J.W. Coop*! He took the time and trouble to fly to Sioux Falls to appear at my stage show at the Farm Show to promote his movie. What a great guy!

I was on security duty one night in 1974, watching a guest house on the Desert Inn Golf Course. Engelbert Humperdinck was staying there with his wife, two boys and one daughter. They were a very nice family who treated me very well.

One night around midnight a lady drove up in a station wagon, looking for a house located just across the street. We had a good visit and she said she would be doing her show at the Desert Inn Resort. It turns out her name was Ginger Rogers.

Yet another night I was on duty at the M.G.M. Grand. I was told to go up to the 21st floor and escort a man down to the showroom. What a gentleman... George Burns.

In 1973 I got a call from Joan Guertin, who was working on publicity for my skydogging show at Las Vegas Downs. She told me to bring Scotty, the Highlander bull, out to the Hacienda Hotel on the Strip for some pictures with a beautiful showgirl. The girl was a tall beauty and just as nice as could be. She got on the bull after petting him. The pictures turned out super and ran in the local paper. This same girl later became the Muriel Cigar girl, then a TV star in the *Cliffhangers* and then a movie star in *Goldengirl*. Her name? Susan Anton.

There was obviously a more sordid side to Las Vegas, as there is to everyday life. But people are more visible and have more at stake there. It seems as if their lives are concentrated, reduced to a shorter time frame, and emotions — high and low — are compressed.

Diary entry dated April 11, 1994, Las Vegas, NV

While working security at the Sportsman, I got acquainted with a woman named "Shawna." She was 39 and living at the Sportsman. I had been single for three years and she really got my attention. We visited each night because she was out and around at all hours. She played all the Las Vegas games ... slots, men and drugs. I wasn't aware of the drugs for a couple of weeks, but then the signs starting showing. She'd call that her "stupid time," and I'm sure that all dopers know it really is stupid. Shawna was very intelligent and was the first to admit what a waste her life had been. I wonder about Shawna a lot. She may be in jail; her lifestyle has many risks and perhaps the least of these is jail time.

Getting to know and care about Shawna reinforces my belief that drugs are not cool and that we don't have enough jail cells for all the pushers, users and producers. We've got to get the message out as early as first grade that drugs are stupid and there is so much more to life than to move through it in a haze.

Chapter 12
Working Girls and Working Guys

Just as there's the glitzy, glamorous side to Las Vegas, I got see plenty of the underworld. It's a seamy life, filled with drugs, prostitution and desperation — as my security partner Eugene and I discovered the hard way.

December nights in Las Vegas are cold. Overnight temperatures dip into the teens but the highs redeem the lows when temps climb to 50 degrees. While I was working security downtown, I was seeing plenty of street life. People often stopped to talk with me and many were lost and lonely. I watched the girls working the streets, but it took me a while to realize what they were doing.

It's rather comical to think how naïve I was back then, thinking the girls standing on the corner at the unemployment office were just waiting to get their checks. A car, van or pickup would stop and they'd talk a little. Usually the girl got in and away they'd go. She's be back to her spot, usually within the hour.

One night a blonde lady was walking close by. She started talking to me and finally I got the nerve to ask her if she was working. She said she was and I asked her how much she charged. She told me that the standard street price was $40. I hastily informed her that I was just curious.

Another girl, about 30, came by many times. She stopped to talk so I asked her how much she charged. She asked, "How much do you want to spend?" Then she saw one of the many unmarked patrol cars and moved on.

It was about 2 a.m. when I first noticed a tall, trim girl with brown hair, dressed in jeans and leather jacket. She was standing across the parking lot from me. She was drinking coffee to combat the freezing cold. Soon a van stopped, they talked a little, she got in and they drove off. Soon the girl was back.

At 4 a.m. I got off duty and stopped. I walked around my pickup and said to the girl I'd noticed during my shift, "Howdy. Are you working?" We discussed money and both got into the pickup. I asked her whether she wanted to go to her place or mine. She said that my place would be fine and asked how far. I told her I had a trailer and lived out at the campgrounds.

She talked as we drove. Her name was Diane and she was an exotic dancer for a Las Vegas club. Dancing was an easy job for a good-looking girl in Vegas because quite a few clubs feature both female and male dancers and strippers.

Diane told me how embarrassed she was the first time she walked out on the stage behind the bar, moving to the music as she stripped off the top of her little outfit. She said she was hesitant to strip the top off but everyone was yelling for her take it off. Finally she did, which must have made for a good show. This became routine for a few weeks and then she said the boss started demanding some action with her. Diane told him to forget it and walked out. She realized that she'd be better off working the streets as an independent than dancing for $25 per shift plus tips.

Back at the trailer, Diane was tired and could hardly keep her eyes open. She told me that she'd smoked some Hawaiian pot and it was really getting to her. I offered her some cookies and a peanut butter sandwich.

She stood up and started taking off her sweater. Diane stepped out of her jeans. Then she looked at me and said, "Pay me first." As I counted out the $35, she asked for another $15 to pay her rent. She also asked if she could stay the rest of the night. I counted out $10 in 50-cent pieces and the rest in quarters.

Diane had hurt her back, she said, falling down some steps. She asked me lie down so she could put her back up against mine to get it warm. She fell asleep and I let her sleep. Eight hours later she stirred and said, "Thanks for letting me sleep." Her sore back had seized up and she couldn't get out of bed. I found some old Ace bandages and wrapped them around her. I helped her dress and then took her out to breakfast.

So ended my first adventure with a working girl!

Working security makes for a lonely life and since I wasn't in a relationship, I had plenty of time to study the habits of working guys and girls. After meeting Diane, I paid even closer attention. All hookers have two or three different names and locations. They keep moving around because they don't want their dates to know where to find them.

I quickly realized that "Diane" was not Diane's real name. She said she was 21 and from California. She was very proud and carried herself with a flair and pride for being independent. Diane was a product of a broken home with little love. She got involved with pot at 9 and by 14 or 15 was a hooker. Diane lived with a boyfriend she thought she loved and walked the streets for him.

She told me that one day she found her boyfriend in bed with two other girls, all high on angel dust. Because of this disgusting experience she refused to get involved with anyone. Of course, nearly every hooker I've talked to has rules against becoming emotionally involved with her date.

Diane had worked around Los Angeles for a couple of years. She dated all types and was involved in everything. She even went out with a TV star now and then. She says that every time she watches the top-rated TV shows she gets a kick out of thinking about the past. Diane was a waitress for a while until she got tired of abuse by customers. Once she dumped a glass of ice water on a smart young man. That cost her the job.

Las Vegas was her next stop. She was the new girl in town and had to fight to stay alive. The cops told her to leave town and the other girls didn't want her occupying their locations. But Diane was determined to stay and she did.

She told me about one date she'd never forget. A nice-looking fellow in a Chevy Blazer pulled up and asked her for a date. He looked and sounded OK to her, so she got into the Blazer and he drove out to a desert lot. She had $300 on her from three dates that evening. "Don't say a word," he warned her, "or I'll blow your head off. I've killed before and one more won't make any difference." He took her money, kicked her out in the desert and drove off.

When I asked Diane about the best date she ever had, she told me about a man who gave her $1,000 for four hours of physical abuse. She said a lot of people are into sado-masochistic sex.

Another time she had a date with five Chinese men. They came up to the room, one after the other and each paid her $100. One night Diane came into the center court of the apartment complex where I was working and told me that a guy, who was up on the second level, was trying to kill her. I met him and he told me Diane was a hooker and had stolen $200 from him the week before. I could see that he'd had too much to drink and I didn't want him to fall off the balcony. So I talked to him and he finally calmed down and left. The next time he saw Diane he apologized. She told me he was just mad because he had wanted a date and she didn't want to go out with him.

Later Diane came over to tell me she had been thrown out of the skating rink. She had hitchhiked down to see me and was clearly high on Quaaludes and booze. She was out of her head and needed $20 to pay her rent. We talked about her crazy lifestyle and she ended up throwing a fit. My security dog started biting her — nothing serious, but enough to shake her up — and I ended up taking 10 minutes off work and driving her back to her motel. I gave Diane $20 and she threw it on the floor. She was just cracking up. I'll never forget the look in her eyes as I left, like shattered glass!

Diane continued to stop by each night I was working. She knew that I was always there, so she brought coffee for us to drink as we walked and talked. Diane told me that most girls share a room, both to combat loneliness and because two girls walking the streets don't get stopped as often as they do alone. Together they smoked a lot of pot and popped pills. Many of their dates provided pot, pills, coke or angel dust. Diane told me she was against heroin, which she called "H." She had tried it once, shooting up in a bathroom. The fan had sounded like a tornado, everything had gone into high gear and she had gone wild. It's easy to see why people jump out of windows when they're on that stuff.

Anyway, I thought Diane had the potential to be an entertainer. I spent three months working up an act with her and teaching her how to ride a motorcycle. The first time she road, I could see she was a natural. She just loved to ride off onto a dry lake bed. Diane said it was better than getting high.

We worked on a stage act that incorporated whips, ropes and guns. I hoped all of this would do some good for Diane. We had an audition at the Sahara Hotel one Monday night. Diane wore a sexy little outfit, which she had used as an exotic dancer. It would have been a good act, but she was nervous and started drinking beer. By the time she was to go on, she was well on her way to being drunk.

We did a showcase at the Sahara in the afternoon and were scheduled to perform again at 1 a.m. I went to pick her up at about 11 p.m. When I got there Diane had already smoked five or six joints. She was with a teenage boyfriend, so he came along. She was so spaced out, that she couldn't perform. And that was the end of Diane's brief career as an entertainer.

I was fascinated by the human interest angle to Diane's story. I decided that I wanted to research and write about working girls. I got my chance to do an in-depth interview one night.

Mitch was playing 21 at the casino most of the night. She was a good-looking lady with a lot of sparkle. I was in the pit doing the drop and the boss and I were talking. He told me she was lots of fun and in town for a week before going back to work at a ranch for three weeks.

Mitch was around the casino for about a week and during that time we became friends. Casino action gets slow around 3 a.m. so we talked. I asked if she would like to have lunch one day and she accepted, so I said I'd meet her at the little cafe two blocks down the street at 1 p.m. I wondered if she'd be there the next day, but she was already sitting in a booth when I walked in. When Mitch had finished her meal, we had iced tea and I asked if she'd like to come over to my apartment for a while. She said OK and when I drove into the complex she mentioned that she had brought a guy home there just the other night.

We settled down in the air conditioning and Mitch drank ice water. I showed her some pictures from my show business days. She enjoyed looking through them and asked a lot of questions. I told her that I'd like ask her a few questions, too, for a book I'd like to write. Mitch thought it was fine.

She was 21 and had been a hooker for five years. Mitch got her start in Denver and lived with a guy for a while. She got pregnant and had a little boy, who now lived with her mother. She worked the Denver streets and got busted many times. She even spent some time in jail once when they busted her date and got him to testify against her.

Then she came to Nevada, where brothels were legal, two years earlier. At the time of the interview, customers were charged $1 per minute. The management and the girls split the money, 50-50. The lady who ran the place collected the money and both management and the girls kept track. Mitch described the brothel as a motel, complete with a bar, lounge and pool. She got her customers by wandering around the bar, talking to the men.

I asked her how many customers she could handle in any given evening. She said she had managed as many as 40 in a night. Did she like her work? Mitch said she did, but she got tired of it and planned to move to a new place up north on the California line.

I mentioned that I had seen her one night in the casino, arguing with an older man. She said he was her husband, but I thought she was kidding. No, she said, she had married the old guy one night. Mitch said her husband didn't care what she did and she only saw him when she came to town.

We finished the interview and Mitch went back to the ranch to work. Then she came in one morning with a girlfriend. They had just driven to town in a Thunderbird with all their possessions. They got a room and played the casino before Mitch flew up to Denver for a visit. She planned to drive up to Idaho to work in hotel, which they'd heard was a good place to make money even if prostitution wasn't legal there.

I was glad to see Mitch again. We had lunch and went over the interview. She said everything was true.

After getting to know Diane and Mitch, I realized that just as there are hundreds of hookers working Vegas, there are hundreds of routes to prostitution. It didn't take me long to notice how many opportunities there were for cocktail waitresses. There was plenty of money to be made in tips because most casinos pull in players with offers of free drinks, but there were lots of contacts with eager men. Like dealers, keno runners and change girls, cocktail waitresses earn a small paycheck. But between tips and dates, an ambitious girl can make a great deal of money. Dates are usually a pre-set deal at a certain price. In fact, many customers think all cocktail waitresses are working for price. They're bombarded with suggestions like: "How much do you charge, baby?" or "My room number is 1313" or "Here's my room key."

Sometimes the pit bosses will set up dates. After a shift where they earned $50 (back in the 1970s) it's tempting to pick up an extra $100 before heading home. You don't have to do this many times a week before you're looking at a tremendous income.

Naturally, a cocktail waitress who isn't interested is in for a lot of harassment. However, serving drinks in a crowded casino is a hard and demanding job. Waitresses learn to handle difficult customers, people who order drinks and then disappear, gamblers who are bitter over losses and even guys who don't tip. Walking around for eight hours in high heels has got to be exhausting enough without dealing with difficult customers, too!

Although my book didn't materialize back then, my respect for working girls certainly did. It has occurred to me many times since then that although I chose a difficult and dangerous profession, there are many others more risky than mine.

Diary entry dated August 21, 1981, Beaver, UT

A female mud wrestling team called the Chicago Knockers have been working lots of fair dates and are going over big. I was booking my stunt show and decided to hop on the mud wrestling bandwagon by having my wife Sylvia and her daughter Crystal mud wrestle on the show. It was real sporting of them to agree to do it.

I booked a show close to Beaver, UT, and sold them the mud wrestling to go with the stunt show. For a warm-up, we booked a night at a Vegas club called the Cow Palace. We set up a plastic mud ring in the back yard of our Las Vegas home and filled it with oatmeal, sand and clay with lots of water. This was where they practiced for the shows.

At the Vegas match, Crystal was pitted against a local lady disc jockey. The winner of two out of three falls was to win $50. It was an even match, but the disc jockey won. Our next booking was in Beaver. When we pulled into town, the first stop was at the newspaper office. Wearing my promoter's hat, I went in to check on the paper's coverage of the upcoming event. The editor told me a lot of the good Mormon people in the area were upset about mud wrestling at their fair. I talked to the fair officials and reassured them that there wouldn't be any problems with the wrestlers or their outfits. The shows were so popular that even good Mormon girls joined in and we all had fun.

Chapter 13

All Work and No Play Makes Jack a Dull Cowboy

Over the years I've had plenty of laughs. Generally speaking, rodeo riders are fun loving folks and enjoy a good time. Here are a few of the incidents that cracked me up or just illustrate the hilarious moments that come along when you least expect them.

Ben Brune had a small rodeo in a small Minnesota town. I was contesting there in the saddle bronc and bull riding events in 1952. Ben's portable chutes were set up on a hay field with ample access to the back side of the bucking chutes.

Three girls were hanging around talking to the cowboys and enjoying the time and place. Ben had some easy bulls to ride at that time. They would just go straight and jump a bit and run off. One of the girls wanted to ride one. So Dennis Reiners and several other cowboys helped her get on one. I'll say this: She had a lot of guts to try one!

The gate came open and the bull took a jump out. Right at the top of the jump the girl fainted and fell off. She wasn't hurt, but I've always wondered if she ever tried another one.

* * *

Gale Anderson had a gorilla costume so convincing that it rivaled anything I've seen in Hollywood. Gale incorporated his gorilla act into every show, sometimes leaping the fence into the grandstand. Spectators would scatter, kids would cry. One of my favorites was when he sat down beside a lady and then hugged her or kissed her. The crowd howled over that one. The other all-time favorite was when he set up a makeshift outhouse in the middle of the action. Gale would keep telling the announcer he had to go the bathroom. The announcer always told him no, that he had an act to do. Finally the announcer would give in, and Gale would walk into the outhouse. There would be this awful commotion and an explosion and toilet paper would fly out the roof. Finally Gale would run out, chased by a gorilla! The fans just cracked up over this act!

* * *

Gary Beall's dad, Bill, worked some of our shows in 1986-87. He helped set up during the stunts. One insight into my persona: I kept my truck polished and clean at all times. It was white and if there was any mud or dust on it, I'd get out the polish and towel and make it shine again. You might say I was a bit obsessive.

During a demo derby the night before our show at a Minnesota fair, we were parked outside the track with our rigs. I had a box on my pickup and Bill wanted to put his lawn chair up on top and watch the derby over the wood fence. That was OK with me.

The next morning I was walking around my truck and took a good look at it. What a mess! Bill had been spitting tobacco juice off the side while watching the derby the night before. That brown, pulpy juice was splattered all along one side of that white pickup. I'm here to tell you that I'd rather clean fresh cow dung or all the mud in the Mississippi delta off a truck than tobacco juice. That was quite a job!

* * *

Every afternoon at 5 p.m. the M.G.M. Grand Resort had the Orange Crush... at least that was what the security officers called it. One of our security posts was at the service elevators on the lowest level of the 21-floor resort. Each day at 5 p.m. the day shift of maids — all outfitted in orange uniforms — would burst out of the six elevators, headed for the time clock and parking lot. The standard admonition when working that post was to stay in the corner to avoid the orange crush.

* * *

Kyle Evans and his band members pulled a good one on me during a 1974 tour across Nebraska. We were driving our pickups and staying within a mile or so of each other. Dee Dee Ortman was with me and she and Kyle were constantly talking back and forth on a hand-held radio. Once in a while I would say something.
This was fun and helped pass the time.

All of a sudden this deep, booming voice comes across the radio, identifying himself as the Nebraska Highway Patrol. "This is a warning to the unit which just passed the intersection of Highway 20. You must stop using your radio for just idle talk or you'll be subject to arrest."

I threw the radio under the seat and told Dee Dee not to say a word. When we stopped at the next truck stop, Kyle asked if we'd heard the Highway Patrol officer. Then he started to grin. Only then did I realize he'd been the voice on the radio!

* * *

I attended the 1993 National Finals Rodeo in Las Vegas as a fan. I had no idea who would be singing the national anthem. How pleased and shocked I was when country superstar and long-time barrel racer Reba McEntire stepped out under the spotlight. I even let out a war whoop!

Diary entry dated November 9, 1969, Sioux Falls, SD

I worked on the indoor Sioux Falls Arena rodeo for years. Along with Don Merrill, Gale Anderson, Bob Kunkel and Jim Sutton, I put a lot of energy into producing the event. The Professional Rodeo Cowboys Association approved the rodeo, so any money won there counted toward the world championships.

This was the pinnacle, if you can accept that word from a flatlander like me, of my producing years. About 4,000 fans attended to see Jay Himes of Beulah, CO, win the bareback riding; John McBeth of Atlanta, KS, win the saddle bronc riding; Ben Calhoun of Canon City, CO, win bull riding; Steve Schultz of New Ulm, MN win the calf roping and (surprise, surprise) Jack McElrath win the steer wrestling event in 3.7 seconds. The fans have made the Sioux Falls rodeo a great professional event and some of my best times were producing the Flying Buckskin Rodeo from 1969 to 1972.

Chapter 14
And the Winner Is...

Everywhere I go, fans ask about the high points of my career. I hesitate to start listing them because I'm not convinced all of them are behind me! That doesn't mean I don't remember the honors, joys and special occasions over the years. But I guess I never thought about an organized recitation of my dubious honors until I read the nomination form my buddy Don Merrill filled out when he nominated me for the South Dakota Hall of Fame.

The form seemed to make sense of my experiences somehow, as if I had planned my life to fall together just the way it has. It's a bit uncanny if you think about it too hard.

Re-reading the list of my memberships brings back a flood of good memories and includes the Professional Rodeo Cowboys Association from 1952 to 1972, the Old Timers Rodeo Association from 1983 to 1988, South Dakota, Iowa and Minnesota State Fair Associations in the 1970s and 1980s, the National Fair Association from 1980 to 1990 and membership in the Michigan Fair Association since 1980.

When Don got to the section about awards and honors, I was humbled. He listed my National Defense Service Medal, winner of the *Super Sports Follies* TV show in 1991, winner of the Great Scott Award in Las Vegas in 1991, the South Dakota Order of the White Buffalo awarded by Gov. Frank Farrar in 1970, my rodeo wins from 1952 through 1988 and more.

But then I had a hearty laugh. Don filled up an entire page under "other pertinent information and comments." I couldn't have found one thing to say there, but Don went on and on. He listed my infamous skydogging "championship," the world record fireslide, host and producer of the *Flying Buckskins* TV show from 1968-1971, producer of the Flying Buckskin Arena Rodeo from 1969-1972, appearing in the movie *J.W. Coop* with Cliff Robertson in 1970 and again at the movie's South Dakota premier in 1971, appearing in the *Thrillseekers* TV show with Chuck Connors, appearing on the *Stuntmasters* TV show in 1991, appearance on *To Tell the Truth* in 1973, the centerfold of the *National Enquirer*, featured in the *Ford Truck Times* in 1968, featured in the *Western Horseman* and *Rodeo Sports News* along with thousands of TV, radio and newspaper articles, and headline act at 500 rodeos and stunt shows from coast to coast for 50 years.

It's amazing what you can do! People who know me well, like Don Merrill, will tell you straight out that I'm constantly amazed by what a person can do if they just set their mind to it and take care of themselves.

I've got to say that when I first began riding my pony at two years of age, I never expected it would come to this: writing about my exploits 60 years later and thinking that people would actually pay good money to read about them!

Diary entry dated October 16, 1996, Sioux Falls, SD

I may have spent $3 to make $2 over the years, but money was never my driving force. Funs and thrills spurred me, along with the quest for an interesting existence. I never dreaded a competition or stunt in my life. I was always excited and even now wake up each morning wondering what new thing I'll experience that day.

I don't believe you could say that I courted danger. I think it's just a partnership you enter into when you choose the lifestyle I did. Risks? Yup, there are plenty. Odds? You bet, I played them. After all, it's no fluke I spent so much time in Vegas.

Chapter 15

Excuse Me, But Did Somebody Mention the Word DANGER?

Of all the stunts I've pulled, all the broncs and bulls I've ridden, and all the cars I've crashed, probably the most dangerous situation of all would have been on a flight over the Pacific Ocean.

I was in the Air Force, returning from Guam in a 124 Globemaster Cargo plane. That plane lumbered along at about 200 miles an hour and the trip seemed interminable. We were 10,000 feet over the Pacific, about half way between Hawaii and Travis Air Force Base just east of San Francisco.

The cargo was in the center of the plane and troops sat in canvas seats running along the sides of the 124, facing the cargo. All at once the cargo elevator broke and fell to the bottom of the hold, knocking the bottom doors part way open. I could look right down between my legs and see the ocean 10,000 feet below.

I wasn't really panicked; this was an exciting new development in an otherwise boring trip. The plane rattled and shook like a barn as it flew through the air and this problem startled me right out of my boredom. Suddenly the load master interrupted my reverie of what-ifs and shouted, "No one move. Sit still and fasten your seat belt. If the cargo falls any more it will pull you right with it." Nobody knew what was going to happen next and all of the possibilities took off with my mind. Nobody said a word as the load master struggled to get the cargo secured with an overhead hoist. This took about half an hour and in the meantime we all just sat there, alone with our thoughts and the clear sight of water far below. And then the excitement was over and we continued on into Travis A.F.B. with the wind in our faces.

I guess you could say that I've always courted danger. You can't work with bulls weighing 1700 pounds or cars that weigh two tons without a healthy dose of danger DNA. But despite the chills, thrills and tumbles, I've only broken a major bone once, and that was during a fair in York, NE, in 1970 when I tried to distract a bull so the cowboy contestant could get away. The black Angus bull pinned my left leg to a plank and broke it. I spent five months on crutches, but the injury healed perfectly.

The left side of my body has taken most of the pounding. My left wrist broke back at Longfellow Elementary School when I jumped and landed wrong. A bull stepped on my left ankle at the Custer, SD, rodeo in 1965. I drove across the state to Sioux Falls before I had a doctor take a look at it. And I cracked my left elbow during a bull-riding event in Spooner, WI, in 1966. A bronc called Cloudy Day retaliated after I won the bronc riding event in 1959 at Menomonie, WI. On my get-off, his hoof connected and knocked out a couple of wisdom teeth. I broke three toes on my left foot during a 1986 Illinois stunt show and Sylvia and I drove all the way to Beaver, UT, before seeing the doctor. That one required a cast for six weeks.

I managed to break a couple of ribs doing the fireslide at the Boone, IA, fair and stunt show in 1989. I also flipped an auto during a big auto jump at the same show. I'm sure that didn't help any! And I was knocked out once during the bronc riding event at Spanish Forks, UT, in 1968. I went on to bulldog a steer and did the Roman riding act, despite my stunned condition.

All in all, I've been very lucky in my concentrated courtship of danger. I'm thankful to have been injured fewer than a dozen times during a 50-year career. Some might say my luck has more to do with a hard head than any real skill!

Diary entry dated January 3, 1991, Las Vegas, NV

The Great Scott Award was a sports show promotion for Channel 8. Scott Higgins was the sportscaster for the station and was on the lookout for interesting sports stories for his portion of the evening news.

I wrote and told him about my 100-foot fireslide. Scott wanted to film it for his show. Sylvia and I went out to the Las Vegas Speedway and set up the fireslide for TV. We shook out a 100-foot-long row of hay and soaked it with five gallons of gas. We torched it and, as I was seated on my old shovel, Sylvia towed me all the way with our pickup. The camera man positioned himself in the pickup bed and really shot some good video.

The show was very interesting and well done. Scott presented us with his "Great Scott Award," and must have liked it well enough to run the video at least 20 times over the years.

Chapter 16
How to Get Your Face on TV

Appearing on TV has never been an accident. Sometimes there is a long chain of events leading up to that appearance, but mostly it's hard work behind the scenes. As I competed over the years, I started paying attention to how promoters did their jobs. Their work is very deliberate; they know who to call, when to call and what to say. I had to learn these skills and tactics in order to promote The Flying Buckskins, and I've applied them throughout my career.

If you do something interesting or have something of interest to say, you can be invited to appear on talk shows and game programs. This concept really hit home for me back in 1973. My skydogging escapade had just aired on CBS News. Paul Harvey had even picked it up. Hard on the heels of that publicity, came an invitation to appear on Gary Moore's popular show, *To Tell the Truth*.

It can be as simple as writing to the show's program director. The name and address are often included on the screen at the end of the show. There is a national publication which lists people and their claims to fame. Many radio and TV bookers depend on this publication. Just contact your local TV station and ask about it; the name has changed over the years.

And don't expect a whopping check when you finally hit pay dirt. I usually got paid union scale plus the plane tickets to wherever the show was filmed. In the case of my *To Tell the Truth* appearance, I got paid $300 plus round-trip air fare from Las Vegas to New York City.

Four Star Productions, which produced the

Thrillseekers TV show, was union. I was paid close to $1,000 for the 1973 location shoot south of Las Vegas. However, the series ran over and over during a seven-year time span. Each time it aired in a new market I was paid a residual of about $300.

I also got paid for the location shoot at Husets Speedway in Sioux Falls, SD, in 1991. *Stuntmasters* paid me $500 total, but I considered the worldwide exposure to be worth much more.

Super Sports Follies may have been the best deal so far. I sent a video of my stunts to an address listed on the show in 1990. In January of 1991 I received a check for $1,000 <u>and</u> they ran the video on the show.

Back when I hosted the *Flying Buckskins* TV series from 1968-1971, I thought I'd landed a major coup. I sold the idea for the show to Mel Heath, program director. Our deal was that I sold the ads and after $100 worth in advertising was purchased, I received 50 percent. Back then ads sold for $10 per 10-second spot. Plus I got the joy of planning and performing.

I've been a guest on more TV news and radio shows than I can remember. Most of the time I was promoting an event. I did a lot of shows in response to an ad in a TV and radio trade paper. Stations called from Boston, Denver, Salt Lake and more. Although there was no money in the appearance, I got a chance to promote my events. This built my reputation and enhanced the frequency of my bookings.

Diary entry dated November 20, 1972, Sioux Falls, SD

I produced the Sioux Falls Rodeo these past four years. The first one, after a year of promotion, was a great production. We had two performances attended by 10,000 people with 200 cowboys and cowgirls competing. We had Sutton's good stock — the best of everything. The frosting on the cake that year was when I won the bulldogging event with a time of 3.7 seconds. It was a good thing I enjoyed myself that night because even though I brought in $25,000, I was broke after paying all the bills. I decided to do better the following years. We had three performances attended by nearly 10,000 people. I fell behind a little on this one, too, mostly because of gifts to charities but hoped to recoup the next year. But I had gotten some poor advice about allowing other professional rodeos even though I had exclusive rights. This diluted my rodeo and the final year only 3,000 attended. So I'm hanging it up and heading for Las Vegas. I'm so far in debt I don't know what to do.

Chapter 17
To Tell a Good Story You've Got to Lead An Interesting Life

I've enjoyed doing stunts — riding saddle broncs, wrestling steers and trying to stay on bulls — since I first burst onto the rodeo scene as a teenager. It's fun, thrilling and the competition has always made it interesting.

If the fear was too great, I don't think you could continue doing stunts. Excitement was my driving factor and I was always excited. I *really* wanted to do the ride or stunt. Of course, I've been very lucky over the years. I've suffered few injuries. Conditioning has a lot to do with my good health, as has desire. This is the life I want. I still feel like doing stunts at 63, so I'll stay in shape and keep on doing them.

The wandering life has brought me in touch with all sorts of people. While I was traveling with the Air Force, carnivals, rodeos and motorsports shows I saw lots of different country, held interesting jobs and met some unusual folks.

One of the more unusual jobs was mining out in the Pan American north of Pioche, Nevada, hometown of Jim Devlin. I worked there during the winter of 1977-78, driving a road scraper and hauling the ore up out of the mine. Each load weighed 80,000 pounds and the mine was a mile deep. That cat V-8 diesel engine would really roar as it pulled the load up that six percent grade to the top of the tunnel. Every day was an adventure at the mine. All the drilling and blasting to bring the hard rock ore down was deafening and my experience heightened my respect for miners.

Utah is a beautiful area and I got to tour parts of it doing rodeo work. My acts at Spanish Forks, Heber City and Logan in 1968 took me through farming and ranching areas. The drylands there give way to winter sports in the Park City resort area.

In 1970 I took a rodeo trip to Moses Lake and Walla Walla, WA. It's a big, open country sparsely populated with ranches. It's memorable because I won over $500 in the steer wrestling competition and had arranged a $500 deal for my acts. My sister Janice Long and her husband Ralph were vacationing there.

Canada, too, is lovely. I worked some rodeos in Armstrong, British Columbia, and Panoka, Alberta. The "B" circuit of fairs in 1978 led me all over the western part of Canada. My act at that time was as a clown on a motorcycle, set on top of a pole rigged up on my horse trailer. I shot arrows at targets and then dropped into a water tank. Dee Dee Ortman, Karla Aman and I used this act at the South Dakota State Fair the same year and with the Murphy Brothers Carnival in Tulsa, Houston and Galveston.

Traveling to fairs, rodeos and carnivals in Wisconsin has enabled me to link up with old friends such as Bette Ketchem at Mauston. Bette lives in a whole other world than I usually encounter — dairy farming. She was a good friend in Sioux Falls in the late '40s and early '50s and we enjoyed the horses. I've contested in and announced at great rodeos like Spooner, Manawa and Darlington. It's great fun to get around because you just never know whether the rodeo will be at a fairgrounds or downtown (Pittsburgh and Chicago). You also never know if the crowd will be huge — there were one million people at the Raleigh, NC, state fair and rodeo one fall — or a small affair.

One of my favorite rodeo runs was to Texas and Louisiana. Back in 1952 when I was 18, Chuck Elshaire, his girlfriend Darlene Smithback and I hit the road in September and October. We were just some broke teenage kids, more desperate than anything, when I entered and won the bull riding events at Ringgold, LA. Luckily I drew two good bulls and then held on with an iron grip induced by being penniless, winning two go-a-rounds and the average, which paid big money — $108.

Louisiana is like a whole different country. There's timber, lowland, lots of water, fishing, and oil rigs. I'll always remember a sign in a Louisiana bar window that said: "No TV, but a good fight each night!"

This Texas-Louisiana run as a teenager is quite a contrast with a trip I took in 1986 at the age of 53. I headed off to Phoenix and picked up a few points in the saddle bronc riding. Then off to Elko, NV, in March for another good saddle bronc ride. I showed up in June to ride in the Newell, SD, and Newcastle, WY, rodeos. I even took first place in the Mesquite, NV, rodeo. All of this qualified me for the finals in Amarillo, that year. I didn't end up going because my security work was too involved. Competing was also expensive and the story of my life: I never had the money I needed to do what I needed to do in the style in which it needed to be done. All in all, with the wins in the saddle bronc rides, combined with all of the motorsports activities, 1986 was quite a year for an old coot!

I enjoyed a run to Colorado and Kansas that Don Merrill and I made in 1952. Evergreen, west of Denver, is a beautiful area. I liked Kansas, too, which is flat and open and allows you to see a long way.

I must admit that of all the places I've been, I still like South Dakota the best. It was my home base back in the 1940s, '50s, '60s and early '70s and I fondly recall many trips with my Ford pickup, small camper and horse trailer. Gas was about a quarter per gallon in 1950 and I mostly slept in the pickup and ate food straight from the store. Costs were low, including rodeo entry fees. I usually spent $10 or $15 per event and could win up to $160, depending on how many contestants entered each event. There were still plenty of summers when I barely made enough money to buy a cup of coffee and enough gas to get home. When I saw the $3.2 million prize money at the National Finals Rodeo in Las Vegas this year, I about fell off my recliner. Who would ever have dreamed of that kind of money? Not me. I can remember being thrilled to win $300 in a weekend.

After traveling around the world for all these years, I've come to realize what a fine place Sioux Falls is. Nevada and Minnesota are close runners-up. South Dakota's also home to plenty of good cowboys and cowgirls. Casey Tibbs, nine-time world champion from Ft. Pierre, SD, is probably the most famous of all. I contested with him many times and even won a few. He was the best saddle bronc rider of all time, and not too shabby as a publicity and promotion man for professional rodeo. I miss him since he passed away at the age of 60.

Oklahoma has its fair share of famous folks, too. Reba McIntire, Jim Shoulders, Ben Johnson and Clem McSpadden are just a few. You know, this sport promotes friendliness. This kinship sets us "alternative" athletes apart from others. There is competition, but it ends when the rodeo wraps up. Almost all of my friends are from this world, and I feel that they're the very best.

I must also give Las Vegas credit for being the entertainment capitol of the world. I preferred the city back in the 1960s and '70s. It's just too big today. There are one million people living in Clark County today, a far cry from the 100,000 living in the valley in the late 1940s. When I first visited, you would have had to count all the horses, cows and wildlife to come up a population of 100,000!

So what's the big attraction? Good climate (except for June, July and August) and clear days with little rain. If it gets a bit windy, people can just pop into a casino. I think the food and shows are the very best in the world. For most folks, a weekend in Vegas is plenty. Some can handle it longer. It really depends on how much control you have.

I've worn my traveling boots for so many years that I sometimes sleep in them. I love going down the road to do a show, whether I'm staying in Super 8s or my camper. The countryside, truck stops, fairgrounds and rodeo arenas are all part of a big show. Throughout my travels, I tried to avoid big cities. I used to drive north over the top end of Lake Michigan in order to avoid Chicago traffic. There's always been plenty of activity on the backroads to keep me amused, and I believe that you'll find the true character of America in small towns, diners and street corners.

Diary entry dated February 22, 1997, Las Vegas, NV

After spending November, December and January in South Dakota, the sunshine and dry desert air of Nevada starts sounding real good. I decided that spending three weeks of February in Vegas had a lot of value. Fun in the sun was what it was all about.

Chapter 18
Recalling Events

The United Airlines airfare from Sioux Falls to Vegas was $218, round trip. Now, that is a bargain. I had a perfect flight to Denver, switching from a 737 to a big DC-10. The plane was brimming with 300 people; I guess Vegas never loses its popularity... especially after a long, hard winter.

It was great to see my two sisters and brothers-in-law again. Ralph and Janice Long have a nice new home 3,000 feet up the mountain at Summerlin. What a great place to stay for most of February!

But I wasn't looking for a refuge, I wanted to get out to visit my friends and see what new construction had popped up during my absence. Having worked security at the Sportsman for five years, I was anxious to see the 500 new rooms they had just completed, bringing the total rooms to 700.

The Boulder Highway and Tropicana looks good with new rooms, pool and landscaping. The name is now Royal Manor and I couldn't miss the new theme, "Knights of Old England." It's full of snowbirds, relaxing near the pool in the 70-degree February weather. They must take the remnants of the sunburn all the way back to Canada!

One of the new security officers, Parry, gave me a full tour and complete rundown on what's been going on. Lee was still running the store at night; we had a great time reliving the times at the Sportsman. Bill House wasn't on security any more, but I had lunch with him and Kathy at the Showboat Resort. Bill's on to computers and going to school to learn how to push the right buttons.

Owner Gary Brannon and sister Kay Blalock and I had lunch at Eastern & Tropicana. Marie Callendar's is a very nice place. It was nice of them to ask me out and they had lots of questions about my new life in Sioux Falls as well as this book.

My ex-wife Sylvia and I had lunch at the Western Casino in downtown Las Vegas. It was nice to talk to her and know that all is well in her life. Having lived in Las Vegas for nearly 25 years, I find it has a hometown feel about it — just like Sioux Falls. It was good to check it out and see all the new resorts. You name it, they're building it in Las Vegas. More than 100,000 rooms are available today.

I especially enjoyed the new Texas Station Resort at Rancho and Lake Mead in North Las Vegas. I really enjoy the Texas theme and all the cowboy stuff. There's even a full size 1968 Cadillac convertible, bright red, right over the indoor bar! Just like Texas, everything is bigger than life.

I also liked the Yellow Rose Cafe. I loved the bacon, eggs, grits, toast and coffee. At $2, it works for me! I also enjoyed watching people play the horses. Fifty big-screen TVs broadcast races from all of the major U.S. tracks.

It occurred to me more than once that maybe playing the tourist was the payoff after all of my years of stunts, rodeos and security work. I know what goes on in the country and now I enjoy being at the right place at the right time.

Ralph Murray had worked with me on security at the Sportsman. He was around 70 then and still very capable of handling any situation. We got together at the Texas Station Resort and talked it all over. He was still working security part-time at the Sportsman. Don Prince took the security chief job when I moved back to South Dakota and he was doing a good job keeping order at the Sportsman. They really have a good team of men there and I salute them all!

I later ran into friend and Metro Police Officer Gordon

Jensen. He stopped to find me one morning at the Texas Station Casino to say hi. He was a regular on the patrol that included the Sportsman. We had had many good visits in the early morning while I worked security. Gordon is over six feet tall and weighs more than 200 pounds. He is quite intimidating, whether inside his squad car or out. I really appreciated his presence on more than one occasion at the Sportsman. Gordon had planned to retire in January but decided to stay on active duty for another year. That was a fairly risky decision as far as I was concerned. Anybody who wears a bullet-proof vest to work every day knows that another 365 days of active duty increases the odds of bodily injury.

I didn't spend all of my time shut up in smoky bars or chowing down on bacon and eggs. There were plenty of early morning runs and walks, during which I mulled over my book. There was a lot of ground to cover — literally and figuratively — and was worried about whether I would be able to get across the richness of my life in 18 chapters and dozens of photos. When you get to be 63, your life seems much too complex to capture in a finite number of pages. It's really hard to describe all my conversations over a cup of coffee, or the thoughts that run through your mind as you drive down another back road on the way from somewhere to someplace else. The telephone lines, trees twisted by wind, blowing tumbleweeds, lovely lakes, roadside stands, people strolling along the sidewalk at a market, the rows and rows of cars parked outside an arena. All of these things weave together the strands of a life and that's pretty darn hard to put down on paper.

Even running down a dry road in Las Vegas, I couldn't help but think about the treacherous footing on ice and snow for the previous 90 days in the severe South Dakota winter. But it seemed a million miles away as I clicked into my eight-minute mile pace. After a week of slow running, it really felt good to banish thoughts of my book and chilly Sioux Falls and run fast and easy.

Running is a big pursuit in Vegas, but then so is everything else. I decided that I'd have to make this a regular trip every January or February. I know I can stay busy playing the horses. I like to pick three horses in each race and bet a box quinella. Any 1-2 of the 3 wins. It costs $6 a race. Pay-offs can be good on this. You have to read and study the Daily Racing Form. All the major casinos have race and sports books. They list all the races and show them on many large TV screens. The girls keep bringing you drinks, whatever you want. Some of the finest looking ladies in the world took my mind off my book, the frozen truck sitting in my driveway back in Sioux Falls and even, temporarily, the horses. Yes, Las Vegas is fun!

My sister asked me to present a review of the *The Cowboy Stuntman*, which by then was practically to the printer, to her church group. I tried to sum up my adventures so far for them, just as I had been doing mentally during my morning runs. I also encouraged them to consider writing their own life stories. I know that no one will, but they would find it a rich and rewarding experience. The stunts and rodeo parts of *The Cowboy Stuntman* make for interesting reading (I hope), but each person has many interesting stories. Most of these will be lost forever if they never get passed on, either in written or spoken words. I wanted to pass on these stories, many of which illustrate an era and time that was special to many of us.

The skydogging stunt is a good example. So much time and energy went into the event. This stunt was performed in three locations and even today has worldwide TV coverage. I was the only stuntman to do the stunt and fans are still talking about it 25 years after the stunt. It was certainly physically taxing and when I watch videos clips I start to feel tired and dusty all over again!

A life that includes the 200-foot fireslide, the steel wall auto crash, bull and bronc rides, fast steer wrestling runs, rodeo announcing and producing, the Flying Buckskin horses and Highlander bull acts, motorsport and country music shows, security work at the Las Vegas resorts, national TV shows, meeting stars and champions and making more than 300 friends in 63 years can be the makings of quite a tale. And yet it was a daunting prospect to put it all down on paper.

It all needed to come together in *The Cowboy Stuntman*. I must admit that I wrote this story twice, logging everything in longhand in notebooks that take up an entire cupboard in my Sioux Falls apartment. There are so many stories that never made it into the book. I vividly recall the time when Don Merrill picked up the frying pan with the handle that turned, dumping our last can of beans on the pickup tailgate. And then there was the time Don and I entered a wild cow riding contest at the Custer, SD, rodeo. Talk about wild times! How about the time we played the song "Red River Valley" on the guitar and banjo for the junior horseman club variety show. They loved it and wanted another song. "Red River Valley" was the only song we knew! One time Don sent $20 to a Texas rodeo location to help me out. That was a lot of money in 1952! I still chuckle when I remember the time we rode our horses 20 miles to Garretson, SD, and camped overnight. His poor horse was so tired it barely made it. I even recall my first pair of custom-made cowboy boots. I wore them out and had them revamped and then Don wore them for a long time after that. I wonder if he thinks of that today when he buys a new pair of boots for $300! Remembering all the events and people makes the years of work that went into *The Cowboy Stuntman* all worth while.

I hope the photos will tell my story better than I can. And maybe my words will answer any questions brought out by the pictures, or perhaps the pictures will answer any questions dredged up by my writing.

There aren't nearly enough photos of the rodeo days. During the 1950s and '60s up till 1972, 90 percent of the rodeos we contested at were Bob Barnes' rodeos. They were in the Upper Midwest and handy to get to. All were R.C.A. approved. Now they've added a "P" in front, making it the Professional Rodeo Cowboys Association.

There were some big rodeos and some small county fairs. All were a lot of fun. We worked one rodeo at a time in those days and thoroughly enjoyed the two or three days at each. I did everything at Barnes' – from contesting to working the labor list. In the 1960s I announced a lot and worked my acts. That was prime time. I know it will never be that great again. The fast pace of today's rodeos can't be much fun.

I told all of these tales to the 20 ladies from my sister's church group, andwhen I came back to the present from my reveries, I was a bit surprised when they each requested a signed copy of my book!

Diary entry dated October 10, 1995, Sioux Falls, SD

Having worked over two years at the Sportsman Resort in Las Vegas without a break, it was time for a vacation. I left Las Vegas on Oct. 7, driving to Utah and traveling Interstate 15 north to Provo then I-89 over to Interstate 80 in Wyoming. It was fun to be back on the road and I took my time driving to Sioux Falls. Taking five days to go 1,500 miles is the way I like to travel.

Chapter 19
This Big Go-Round Called Life

My magical traveling boots had brought me back to Sioux Falls just in time for the long, hard Midwestern winter. Don and Alyce Merrill were glad to see me and I enjoyed being back in this good location, a city of 100,000 with a good trade area. I checked around and came up with a security job, put in for my Social Security and decided to stay for a while. A nice apartment rounded out the new lifestyle and I was all set to face the cold.

As I hunkered down with my job, my buddies, and my steaming cup of Earl Grey, I got to thinking about the many people who have passed through my life in the past 63 years. All, from celebrities to my classmates, have played an important role in who I am today. My heartfelt thanks go to:

- Don and Alyce Merrill, long-time friends who rodeoed and ranched near Canistota, SD, and now live in Sioux Falls, SD
- Gale and Avis Anderson, who worked the shows for years as a rodeo clown, from Tea, SD
- Gary Beall, a stuntman who worked many shows with me, from Santa Fe, TX
- Bob and Donita Barnes, rodeo producers whose shows I worked many years, from Peterson, IA
- Kenny and Barb Carlson, rodeo buddies since 1950, from Alden, MN
- Cotton Rosser, owner of the Flying - U- Rodeo from Marysville, CA
- Casey Tibbs, perhaps the greatest saddle bronc rider of his time, from Ft. Pierre, SD

- Dennis Reiners, world champion saddle bronc rider in 1970, from Phoenix, AZ, and Clara City, MN, the only world champion cowboy from Minnesota
- Doug (9-Toes) Marble, a Harley Davidson motorcycle stuntman from Mankato, MN
- Jim Perrin, a monster truck show producer, of Newaygo, MI
- James Sutton, rancher, cowboy and owner of Sutton Rodeo Co., of Onida, SD
- Jim and Julie Sutton, ranchers and rodeo producers from Onida, SD
- Steve Sutton, cowboy, rancher and stock contractor from Onida, SD
- Jerry and Fern Olson, rodeo clown who had many special acts and rancher from Fruitdale, SD
- Kyle Evans, a singer who was a great help on the show, of Wessington Springs, SD
- Jim and Bonnie Jones, nice people and all-around cowboy, of Akron, CO
- Mel and Wendy Potter, rodeo contestants and friends from Marana, AZ
- Ralph Murray, a security buddy from Las Vegas, NV
- Dee Dee Ortman, who performed in my show, of Canistota, SD
- Merl and Hazel Ostgaard, junior horsemen club advisors from Sioux Falls, SD
- Tanya and LaCosta Tucker and their parents Beau and Juanita of Brentwood, TN, who have great talent and never forgot Buckskin Jack
- Fred and Sharon Peterson, farmers and rodeo contestant of Flandreau, SD
- Jim and Sherrie Devlin, who did stunts and construction and worked many of my shows, from Las Vegas
- Johnny Airtime, a motorcycle stuntman who was featured often on the *Stuntmasters* show, of Las Vegas, NV

- Frank Farrar, former governor of South Dakota, who now lives in Britton, SD, and who, at the age of 67, still competes in the Ironman Triathlon events
- Chuck and Sparky Dent, rodeo contestants and trick riders from Vero Beach, FL
- Lucky Lott, an all-time major player in the thrill show world, of Ontario, Canada
- Barbara Mandrell, a singer and entertainer who made me feel like part of her family, of Nashville, TN
- Dean Martin, singer and star, of Hollywood, CA
- Dottie West, a singer and entertainer, of Nashville, TN
- Herb Alpert, a friendly band leader, of Hollywood, CA
- Cliff Robertson, movie star and great guy from Hollywood, CA
- Ray and Joanie Kelly, artists and announcers who worked my shows, from Tea, SD
- Neil and Bonnie McElrath, my brother and his wife from Rancho Mirage, CA, and their children Steve, Meg, Mike, Richard, Karen, Tim, Tom, Mark and Mary
- Glenn Wentzel, a great booster and friend who helped with video and film for my shows, from Sioux Falls, SD
- Doris and Vince O'Connell, my sister and brother-in-law who are good Iowa farmers in Oto, IA, and their children Marcia, Dennis and Bill
- Janice and Ralph Long, sister and brother-in-law who are great fans and help to me and who love living in Nevada
- Bob and Carol Logan, who farmed and worked construction way back to 1933, from Moville, IA
- Gina Campbell, singer, horsewoman and Miss South Dakota 1976 who worked my shows, from Canton, SD

- Kitty Halde McElrath, super horsewoman and my first wife, from Sioux Falls, SD
- Duane Howard, P.R.C.A. champion and No. 2 bull rider twice, of Minnewaukan, ND
- Liz Gregory, a talent agent who booked my show, from Tualatin, OR
- Karen Seefong McElrath, another good horsewoman who was my second wife, of Canton, OH
- Misty Baugher, who worked in the Sportsman office in Las Vegas, NV
- Bette and Gene Riddlestene, formerly of Sioux Falls, now of Mauston, WI
- Karla and Jeff Laackman, who worked my shows, of Isanti, MN
- Rolly Samp, a long-time advisor who helped on many shows as well as this book, of Sioux Falls, SD
- Denny Oviatt, an announcer who worked many of my shows, of Sioux Falls, SD
- Sylvia Garbati McElrath, a great lady and my third wife, of Las Vegas, NV
- Bill House, a security buddy from Las Vegas, NV
- Liz Olsen, a stunt woman who worked many of my shows, from Las Vegas, NV
- Quail and Judy Dobbs, a clown who worked with me a lot, of Coahoma, TX
- Bob Kunkel, the Arena manager and a great help, of Sioux Falls, SD
- Cliff Foss, pilot for my skydogging stunt, of Sioux Falls, SD
- "Shawna," a Las Vegas friend who helped me out many times
- Lee Meredith, who was THE BEST and who worked with me at the Sportsman store in Las Vegas, NV
- Ben Brune, the rodeo producer who began my career, of Sioux Falls, SD

- Clem McSpadden, announcer at the Sioux Falls rodeo, former state Senator and P.R.C.A. National Finals C.E.O., of Chelsea, OK
- Johnnie Jackson, announcer and producer who invited me out to his rodeo in Woodlake, CA
- Ray Brooks, a farmer, lifelong friend and owner of a Sioux Falls, SD, construction company where I worked from 1949-51
- Clyde and Ruth McElrath, my great folks who farmed and raised livestock near Moville, IA, and later lived in Sioux Falls
- Don Prince, a security buddy from Henderson, NV
- Gordon Jensen, Metro Police officer from Las Vegas, NV
- Darrell Sorenson, pilot for my Las Vegas, NV, skydogging stunt
- Dean Tabke, livestock man, cowboy and trucker from Canistota, SD
- Fred and Catherine Halde, lath and plaster contractors and my former in-laws from Sioux Falls, SD
- Frank and Lulu Clapper, junior horseman club advisors of Sioux Falls, SD
- Kenny and Webe Thompson, horseman and horse racer from back in 1957, from Sioux Falls, SD
- Dave Mason, who announced many of my shows, of Jefferson, WI
- Roy Coffman, motorsports and rodeo announcer from Omaha, NE
- Babe Cox, a cowboy, livestock and rodeo man from Knoxville, IA
- Marge Hokenstad, who was a great help on my TV show, of Sioux Falls, SD
- Myles Johnson, fair secretary who lent much assistance, of Spencer, IA

- Jack Hunter, rancher, announcer and sound man from Armour, SD
- Steve and Marie Brand, stunt people who worked my shows, of Wichita, KS
- Gilbert Slemin, a motorcycle stuntman, of Williston, ND
- C.T. Jones, a cowboy and rodeo contestant, of Jonesboro, AR
- Jeff Werner, who did the photo shoot for the *National Enquirer*, of Hollywood, CA
- Francis Misgen, a great help with my stunt cars, of New Richland, MN
- Alison Bly, a/k/a the Dynamite Lady, of Tampa, FL
- Albert Carollo, fair member who was a great help, of Norway, MI
- Ole Anderson, stuntman from Neola, UT
- Tom and Hazel Drake, good booking agents from Kansas City, MO
- Gale Frost, State Fair historian of St. Paul, MN
- George Moffett, booking agent for Variety Attractions, of Zanesville, OH
- Mike Barr, booking agent, of Zanesville, OH
- Dean Kjelden, a great boss from Ben Hur Ford in Sioux Falls, SD
- Steve Kelly, a stuntman from Springfield, MO
- Bob Bennis, a great boss at Ben Hur Ford, of Brandon, SD
- Randy Gilbert, general manager of Menards, Sioux Falls, SD
- Dr. Louis Allgeyer, fair secretary and great help from Owatonna, MN
- Spanky Spangler, a stuntman of Phoenix, AZ
- Bill Wales, a construction buddy from Sioux City, IA
- Charles Belknap, of the Hollywood auto stunt show in Tampa, FL

- Herman Gumper, fair secretary at a great fair we worked in Jackson, MI
- Gerald Munns, fair secretary of Rock Rapids, IA
- Winston Bruce, champion saddle bronc rider and rodeo manager from Calgary, Canada
- Scott Higgins, who showed the fireslide video on his Channel 8 sports show in Las Vegas, NV
- Ratt Reno, KXRB radio personality of Sioux Falls, SD
- Duane Reichert, a rodeo clown from New Underwood, SD
- Steve Rubin, from Husets Speedway and *Stuntmasters* TV video, of Sioux Falls, SD
- Olive Manlet, security buddy and manager of the Guinness Museum in Las Vegas, NV
- John Kroll, producer of the *Stuntmasters* TV show, of Studio City, CA
- Merritt Triggs, fair manager of Mt. Ayr, IA
- Ed Beckley, motorsports show producer of Wichita, KS
- Wendy Kenney, booster, buddy and bartender from Las Vegas, NV
- Mark and Mary Adams, contractor and sponsor of Sports Day in Canistota, SD
- Dwight McLaughlin, a buddy from Columbus, OH, who visited me in Las Vegas
- J.W. Stoker, a trick roper who worked in rodeos and movies, of Weatherford, TX
- Sheldon Songstad, owner of Buffalo Ridge Old West Town near Sioux Falls, SD
- LaWanda Linsey, a singer from Bakersfield, CA, who worked with me
- Bob Hansen, an auctioneer from Salem, SD
- Gene and Carol Campbell, cowboy contestant, of Rochester, MN

- Dan Barrett, rodeo contestant and fair board member of York, NE
- John Walters, a rodeo producer from Kirksville, MO
- Josette Van Hise Rogers, a fan, booster and buddy from Las Vegas, NV
- Merl Miller, an auctioneer from Wall Lake, SD
- Ron Spicer, a rodeo contestant from Rochester, MN
- Lola Jean Dillon, a singer who worked many of my shows, of Nashville, TN
- Pam Martin Minick, a cowgirl, TV announcer and Miss Rodeo America, of Ft. Worth, TX
- Ed Pillar, a showman, booster and horseman from Scotland, SD
- Frank Strout, a cowboy from Selma, AL
- Tommy Lucia, a rodeo clown from Minneapolis, MN
- Leon Adams, a rodeo contestant from Stuart, OK
- Ted and Rhoda Warhoe, one of the first PRCA members who rodeoed and raced horses, from Minneapolis, MN
- Jim and Donna Prestine, rodeo contestants from Denver, IA
- Erv Korkow, stock contractor and rodeo producer from Blunt, SD
- Jim Korkow, stock contractor and rancher from Blunt, SD
- Albert Weisel, producer of Crystal Springs Ranch Rodeo in Clear Lake, SD
- Chuck and Dit Elshaire, rodeo contestants from South Shore, SD
- Lowell James, rodeo contestant who competed in the National Finals Rodeo and casino dealer from Las Vegas, NV
- Jimmy Schmaucher, rodeo clown and casino dealer from Las Vegas, NV

- Connie Griffith, a trick rider at Excalibur Resort in Las Vegas, NV
- JoAnn McEninney, a trick rider from Tarkio, MO
- Janette Plunket, a trick rider from Kansas City, MO
- Neil Samules, a rodeo contestant and western clothing salesman from Omaha, NE
- Johnnie Galvin, a band member and singer of *I Washed My Face in the Morning Dew*, of Bushnell, FL
- David Firestone of Palm Desert, CA
- Vern Whitaker, rodeo contestant whose son Chip was an all-around cowboy, of O'Neill, NE
- George Doke, a rodeo clown from Fort Worth, TX
- Dittman Mitchell, a rodeo announcer from Kansas City, MO
- Dusty Lee Rivers, a singer and stuntman from Winnipeg, Ontario
- Joan Guertin, a public relations pro and horse person from Las Vegas, NV
- Susan Anton, actress and Miss California, of Hollywood, CA
- Bill Linderman, an all-around great cowboy from Red Lodge, MT
- Walt Linderman, steer wrestler whose horses I rode to wins, from Red Lodge, MT
- John Christopherson, a steer wrestler whose son Bob is a great cowboy, too, from Sioux City, IA
- Swanney Kirby, a stock contractor of Salt Lake, UT
- Bunky Boger, a rodeo clown from Springdale, AR
- Earl Borneman, a cowboy who had stables on 41st Street in Sioux Falls, SD
- Hank Metzger, a horseman who operated the junior horseman arena on 41st Street in Sioux Falls, SD
- Donna, Nancy, Jeff and Jamie Merrill, my buddies from Sioux Falls, SD

- Mark Fish, Joie Chitwood Stunt Show announcer from Tampa, FL
- Crystal Edwards, who did stunts in my show in 1983-84, from Las Vegas, NV
- Shawn and Brian Edwards, stuntmen who also worked security in Las Vegas, NV
- Bob Jackson, promoter for Murphy Brothers Shows in Tulsa, OK
- Jim Moreau, stuntman from Bangor, ME
- Lyle and Gay Booth, who provided sound for fairs and rodeos, from Cherokee, IA
- M.D. Thunder Klunder, who had the Motordome Thrill Show, from Minneapolis, MN
- Bill Ruport, who performed in motorsports shows, of Minneapolis, MN
- Byron Whaler, a horseman from Sioux Falls, SD
- Dick and Connie Lacey, farmers from Sioux Falls, SD
- Ralph and Herb Hoffman, horsemen and saddle club members from Sioux Falls, SD
- La Rue Olson, who showed a buffalo act, from Whitewood, SD
- Les Hammer, a horseman and stables owner from Sioux Falls, SD
- Jack and Ellen Paulton, ranchers from Custer, SD
- Dean Hansen, a construction buddy from Sioux Falls, SD
- Pete Congar, a biker from Las Vegas, NV
- Charlie Haegle, saddle shop owner in Sioux Falls, SD
- Don Cook, a horseman and Realtor in Sioux Falls, SD
- Bill and LaVerl Van Wyke of Haegles Western Store in Sioux Falls, SD
- Mort and Sylvia Henkin of KSOO Radio and TV in Sioux Falls, SD

- George Merrill, a horseman and saddle club advisor in Sioux Falls, SD
- Mike McElrath, who worked my shows as a clown, from Palm Desert, CA
- Tim Bare, a cowboy and rodeo stock contractor from Peoria, IL
- Eddie Boysen, cowboy announcer and trick roper from Sioux Falls, SD
- Marty, John and Mitzi Barnes, children of Bob and Donita Barnes and rodeo producers from Peterson, IA
- Joe Darst, a construction buddy from Sioux Falls, SD
- Dick Haynes, a construction buddy from Sioux Falls, SD
- Bill Atterbury, a stuntman and performer in the 60-foot sway pole act, from Las Vegas, NV
- Mark McElrath, a great little cowboy back in 1960, from Sioux Falls, SD
- Tex Flynn, a cowboy and rodeo contestant from Eau Claire, WI
- Carl Dunsing, a security buddy and carnival man from Worthing, SD
- Austin Merrill, my two-year-old buddy from Sioux Falls, SD
- Jordan, Isaac and Taryn Gerdes, children of Mark and Nancy Gerdes, Sioux Falls, SD
- Jerry Meyers, horseman and member of the Sioux Falls junior saddle club
- Sandy Bush, junior saddle club member from Sioux Falls, SD
- Mary Lu Clapper, junior saddle club member from Sioux Falls, SD
- Curt Farstad, manager of the Starlight Drive-in back in the '50s in Sioux Falls, SD
- Bob Portice, a good school buddy from Sioux Falls, SD

- Terry Etzhorn, a cowboy and rodeo contestant from Fort Pierre, SD
- Eugene Bradford, my security buddy who was killed in a bar holdup in Las Vegas, NV
- Bonnie Nelson, a singer in my show from Nashville, TN
- Roy Miller, a horseman, author and poet from Custer, SD
- Benny Reynolds, an all-around cowboy from Roundup, MT
- Erv and Arleen Ortman, doctor, horseman and rancher from Sioux Falls and Canistota, SD
- My niece Pat Barnhill and her children David, Ruthanne and Ronald of Las Vegas, NV
- Susan Rosenbaum, a security buddy from Sioux Falls, SD
- The Flying Buckskins, otherwise known as Bob, Buck, Champ and Tag, from Sioux Falls, SD
- Larry and Kandis Brighton, managers of the Sportsman Resort in Las Vegas, NV
- Verlyn Hofer, who printed my show posters, from Lennox, SD
- Pat Kerby, a video producer from Las Vegas, NV
- Mike Shane and Terry McDonald, Expo of Wheels in Ajax, Ontario
- Linda Scheil, bartender at the Sportsman Resort in Las Vegas, NV
- Wendell Anderson, *Canistota Clipper* newspaper in Canistota, SD
- Randy Hascall and Steve Young of the *Argus Leader* newspaper in Sioux Falls, SD
- Walt and Brenda Winter, security buddies from Las Vegas, NV
- Norris Thune, fair secretary in Thief River Falls, MN

- Lyle Hindes, maker of signs and flags in St. George, UT
- Montie Montana, a cowboy trick roper from Hollywood, CA
- Shawn and Lorie Edwards, stuntman and security guard from Henderson, NV
- Steve Rotfeld, producer of Super Sports Follies who awarded $1,000 prize earnings from Bryn Mawr, PA
- Marty and Kate Davis, singer and band member from Medford, OR
- Laura Schwarz of *Stuntmasters* TV show in Studio City, CA
- Max Willis, manager of International Association of Fairs in Springfield, MO
- Judd and Janine Nielsen of the Total Stop Store in Canistota, SD
- Kathleen Love, model, actress and trade show narrator from Las Vegas, NV
- Douglas MacValley, stuntman from Las Vegas, NV
- Trish Quinn of the Sportsman office in Las Vegas, NV
- Maurice Nelson, farmer and fan from Viborg, SD
- Steve and Kim Hedden, stuntman from Waco, NE
- Jeff and Tracey Merrill, lifelong buddy and son of Don and Alyce Merrill, of Baltic, SD
- Tina and Gary Desch, buddies from Boulder Station in Las Vegas, NV
- Sherry and Mike Potter, PRCA member and world champion barrel racer from Mariana, AZ
- Wayne Divorak, horseman and contractor from Sioux Falls, SD
- Warren Friessen, contractor and great help on Arena rodeo in Sioux Falls, SD
- Ray Dunkelberger, horseman and father to rodeo family including Connie, Larry and Ronnie from Sioux Falls

- Jeri Cunningham, manager of the Western Mall in 1976, Sioux Falls, SD
- Gary Brannon, owner and manager of the Sportsman Resort in Las Vegas, NV
- Shane and Lex Anderson, lifelong buddy and rodeo clown from Kirksville, MO
- Shane, Travis, Carl and Troy Anderson, sons of Gale Anderson from Sioux Falls, SD
- John and Judy Lynn Kelly, singer and booking agent from Las Vegas, NV
- Joyce Rice, cowgirl, singer and showperson who worked my 1971 Sioux Falls Arena show from Goodlettsville, TN
- Mel Heath, manager of KSOO and director of my TV show in Sioux Falls, SD
- Rhonda Sedqwick, musician, horsewoman and rancher from Newcastle, WY
- Bob Gardner, cowboy and owner of Hale Horse Trailers of Sioux Falls, SD
- Jerry Jewel, great rodeo fan from Sioux Falls, SD
- Bob Jamison, rodeo booster and longtime friend to Don and me from Sioux Falls, SD
- Chuck Gardner, New York Life representative and booster from Sioux Falls, SD
- Jerry Cordell, musician and singer from Sioux Falls, SD
- Clark Butler, western wear representative from Sioux Falls, SD
- Jerry Wayne Olson, who worked rodeos from Fruitdale, SD
- Roger Minor, Billie Howalt, Trudy Aker, Mark Stavig, Richard Assam, Jenny Boersma, Marlene Dietrich, Selda Jane Lacey, Don Malcomb, Nancy Nystrom, John Peckham, Alonzo Smith, Mary Woods, Tom Lemonds,

Dianne Green, and Onealee Parsons, school buddies and members of the Washington High School Class of 1952, Sioux Falls, SD

- LeRoy Van Dyke, cowboy auctioneer and singer from Sedalia, MO
- Jan Freed, author of the *Texas Way* and others who gave me words of encouragement with this book, from Sugarland, TX
- Jaciel Keltgen-Pierson, editor of *The Cowboy Stuntman* from Sioux Falls, SD
- Stan Cadwell, publisher of *The Cowboy Stuntman* and owner of Rushmore Publishing of Sioux Falls, SD
- Delton and Darleen Galoway, trick ropers who worked many of my shows, from Abilene, TX
- Jay Montanna, trick roper with the show in 1974-75 from Las Vegas, NV
- Benny "Boom Boom" Koske, the Human Bomb in the 1986 Astrodome from Tampa, FL
- "Reckless Rex" Phelps, who worked the Astrodome with me in 1986 and who performed the 360-degree aerial motorcycle flip, from Spokane, WA
- Chuck Strange, who jumped 17 autos, ramp to ramp, at the Astrodome in 1986, who hails from Lake Forest, CA
- Catherine Bach, star of *Dukes of Hazzard* TV show who visited with me many times backstage at the M.G.M., from Faith, SD
- Rex and Wanda Rossie, trick riders, ropers and stunt doubles who worked many Barnes' rodeos with me, from Henderson, NV
- Dave Dedrick, who invited me many times to guest star on his *Captain 11* show in Sioux Falls and who worked my Arena rodeo as a special guest
- Kay Bleakly, Barnes Rodeo buddy and professional

rodeo officer from Colorado Springs, CO
- Charlene Howard, who worked with me at the Western Casino in Las Vegas, NV
- Benny Van Cleve, a cowboy contestant from Minneapolis, MN
- Dave Cornel, a horse player from Las Vegas, NV
- Kay Blalock, manager of the Royal Manor in Las Vegas, NV
- Kandi Lee White, a country singer from Las Vegas, NV
- Steve Hedden, stuntman from Waco, NE
- "Hap" Peeples, country booking agent from Kansas City, MO
- Ted and Marcia Smalley, good rodeo buddies from Burkburnett, TX
- Ben Kringen, outstanding livestock and horse man, Baltic, SD
- Lee Miller, horseman from Sioux Falls and Canistota, SD
- Donna Hanson Milner, trick rider from Alexandria, MN
- Velda Brune, trick rider from Sioux Falls, SD, now of Springfield, MO
- Doug Main, cowboy from Sioux Falls, SD, now of Branson, MO
- Don Williams, horseman from Sioux Falls, SD
- Clair Dunkelberger, horseman from Sioux Falls and Tea, SD
- Ken Barnes, rodeo contestant from Cherokee, IA
- Marge Barnes, rodeo contestant from Cherokee, IA
- Wayne Curtiss, cowboy from Sioux Falls, SD, now of Jamestown, ND
- Doug Ihnen, security officer from Sioux Falls and Parker, SD
- Houston Haugo, banker and horseman from Sioux

Falls, SD
- Denny Barnes, bull rider from Sioux Falls, SD
- Gary Barnes, bull rider from Sioux Falls, SD
- Mike Schirmer, former Sioux Falls mayor
- Gordon Peacock, horseman from Sioux Falls and Onida, SD
- Lanny Getzen, horseman from Sioux Falls, SD
- Smokey Jensen, cowboy from White River, SD
- Don Stich, fan from Sioux Falls, SD
- Roger Gravelle, cowboy from Canistota and Faith, SD
- Duane Spader, booster from Sioux Falls, SD
- Johnny Galvin, musician from Bushnell, FL
- Woody Wilson, horseman from Sioux Falls, SD
- Gene Erps, fan from Sioux Falls, SD
- E.W. Smith, horseman from Sioux Falls, SD
- Sandy Reinhardt, singer from Valentine, NE
- Sam Pfeiffer, booster from Sioux Falls, SD
- Paul Ortman, sportscaster from Sioux Falls, SD
- Helen Tabke, longtime family friend from Moville, IA, and Canistota, SD
- Diane Erickson, fan and friend from Canistota, SD
- Gala Evans, horse trainer from Dell Rapids, SD
- Christie and Mike Olson, horse trainers from Dell Rapids, SD
- Barney Boes, boxing instructor and friend from Sioux Falls, SD
- Mark Ovenden, sportscaster who understands the value of a good story, from Sioux Falls, SD
- Mickey Merrigan, horseman from Canistota, SD
- George Mammenga, farmer from Canistota, SD
- Rich Mayer, banker from Canistota
- Roy Rogers – movie, TV star and my boyhood hero – who rode with me in a parade in Victorville, CA, in 1970
- Wayne Newton, horseman and entertainer of Las Vegas, NV.

 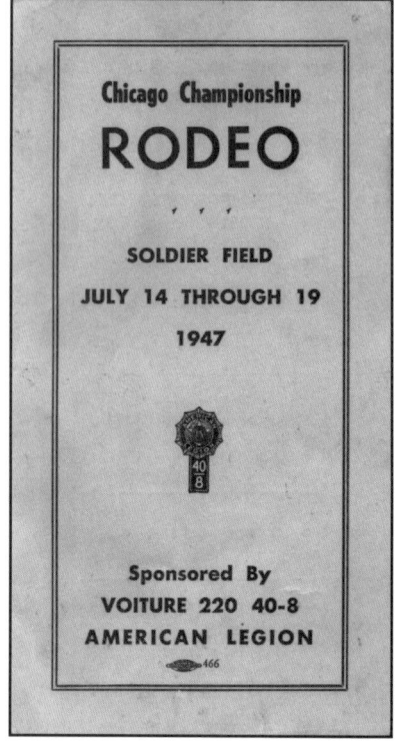

Top left: Casey Tibbs and rodeo are synonymous in South Dakota. Casey was honored at the this banquet in 1950. Clair Dunkelberger saved the program for nearly 40 years.

Top right: It's amazing how a big a rodeo and how much prize money was available in 1947. Prize money was $2200 in each of the five events. Ben Brune was the stock contractor for this rodeo.

All photos from Clair Dunkelberger's' collection

The Cowboy Stuntman

COWBOY UP – COWBOY DOWN

Another city, another state, another gate.
I stand in line, I pay my fees, my achin' back, my achin' knees
I got my number, I got my pride, I draw the bull that I shall ride.
My seat feels good, my hats on tight, I'm good and ready, my rope is right.
"I'm ready boys," now lets begin, the bull, the rider, now which will win.
Gate opens wide, bull charges out, I hear the people scream and shout.
The bull goes left as I go right, now I begin my downward flight.
I see the sky, I taste the mud, I feel the pain, I see the blood.
The clowns rush out, divert the bull, I didn't ride eight seconds full.
The buzzer blares while I am down, I should be up to hear that sound.
I'm dazed and hurt, where is that clown, I'm cowboy up, I'm cowboy down.
So many falls, so many fears, so many pains, so many tears.
The time to quit has come around, I'm cowboy up, I'm cowboy down.
Oh well -----
There's always -----
Another city, another state, another bull, another gate...

Edward R. Cook 96©
Art by Ray Kelly

NOW AVAILABLE
Signed Copies of Author Buckskin Jack McElrath Book
The Cowboy Stuntman

Quantity	Description	Price Each	
	The Cowboy Stuntman	$9.95	
	Subtotal		
	S.D. Residents add 6% Sales Tax		
	$4.00 Shipping & Handling		
	Grand Total		

We Accept MasterCard, Visa, Check or Money Orders.
Send to:

RUSHMORE HOUSE PUBLISHING
P.O. Box 1591
Sioux Falls, SD 57101
(605) 334-5253
1-800-456-1895